"There aren't too many times when the word 'hero' is appropriately used. Heroes are people who do extraordinary things in the service of others. Edgar Harrell is a true American hero."

—Mike Huckabee, former governor of Arkansas,
host of national television and radio shows,
and bestselling author

"*Out of the Depths* is a remarkably moving, moment by moment account of the valor, sacrifice, and faith of the crew aboard the USS *Indianapolis*. David Harrell honors his father, Edgar Harrell, a soft-spoken, reflective veteran of that heroic tragedy, by relating his father's story. As I tried to do in my own book, *When Hell Was in Session*, Mr. Harrell splices and binds the connection and interdependence between courage in the face of death and spiritual faith.

"The saying 'there are no atheists in foxholes' may indeed be a cliché, but it bears more than a kernel of truth. This book makes clear there aren't many atheists, either, in the middle of the Pacific, when your ship is thousands of feet below you, sharks are tugging at your shipmates' legs in the middle of the night, and you are imploring the sailor clinging to you, whom you met for the first time minutes after the explosion, to keep breathing and hanging onto the flotsam for just a little longer—that is, to have the faith to survive.

"It is a harrowing account of the sacrifice of sailors and Marines who fought and died for their country, so we could live. It is a story you should not and will not ever forget."

—Jeremiah A. Denton Jr., RAdm, USN (Ret.)

"I am deeply grateful to Edgar Harrell and the United States Marine Corps. If our nation needs anything at this moment, it is the boost of stories of heroism, courage, and faith. Harrell's unique description of being aboard the torpedoed *Indianapolis* in wartime and his experiences with the treacheries of the deep make an incomparable read. Brimmed full of illustrations of God's graciousness and goodness even amidst incredible suffering, *Out of the Depths* ought to be read by every serious American."

—Paige Patterson, President, Southwestern Baptist
Theological Seminary

OUT OF THE DEPTHS

AN UNFORGETTABLE WWII STORY
OF SURVIVAL, COURAGE, AND THE SINKING OF
THE USS *INDIANAPOLIS*

EDGAR HARRELL, USMC
WITH DAVID HARRELL

BETHANY HOUSE PUBLISHERS
a division of Baker Publishing Group
Minneapolis, Minnesota

Published by Bethany House Publishers
11400 Hampshire Avenue South
Bloomington, Minnesota 55438
www.bethanyhouse.com

Bethany House Publishers is a division of
Baker Publishing Group, Grand Rapids, Michigan

Printed in the United States of America

Library of Congress Cataloging-in-Publication Data
Harrell, Edgar
    Out of the depths : an unforgettable WWII story of survival, courage, and the sinking of the USS Indianapolis / Edgar Harrell, USMC with David Harrell
        pages cm
    Includes bibliographical references.
    Summary: "A WWII hero's courageous, inspiring true story of survival against all odds after the sinking of the USS *Indianapolis*"— Provided by publisher.
    ISBN 978-0-7642-1260-4 (cloth : alk. paper)
    1. Indianapolis (Cruiser) 2. World War, 1939–1945—Personal narratives, American. 3. Shipwreck survival—Pacific Ocean. 4. Sailors—United States—Biography. 5. Marines—United States—Biography. 6. United States. Marine Corps—Biography. 7. World War, 1939–1945—Naval operations, American. 8. Christian biography—United States. I. Harrell, David, Pastor. II. Title. III. Title: Unforgettable WWII story of survival, courage, and the sinking of the USS Indianapolis
    D774.I5H37 2014
    940.54′5973092—dc23   2013047196
    [B]

This book recounts events in the life of Edgar Harrell according to the author's recollection and from the author's perspective. While all the stories are true, some dialogue and identifying details have been changed to protect the privacy of those involved.

Cover design by Paul Higdon

Author is represented by Walter Scott Lamb

14 15 16 17 18 19 20   7 6 5 4 3 2 1

Dedicated to my shipmates,
the crew of the USS *Indianapolis*

Contents

Foreword

"Have courage! It is I. Do not be afraid."

Matthew 14:27 NCV

When that command was issued more than twenty centuries ago, it was to a group of fearful men in peril on a dark and dangerous sea. No exhortation is more appropriate to this chronicle than those words of Jesus Christ.

Shortly after midnight on July 30, 1945, just weeks before the end of World War II, the Japanese submarine *I-58* launched a spread of torpedoes at the USS *Indianapolis*. Two of the "fish" found their mark. In less than fifteen minutes, the heavy cruiser—a battle-scarred veteran of the bloody campaigns for the Marianas, Iwo Jima, and Okinawa—went down without a trace, and without anyone but the survivors knowing the ship had been lost.

Some nine hundred of the ship's 1,196-man crew—cold, oil soaked, many with injuries—were suddenly alone in the shark-infested waters of the Philippine Sea. For five horrific days after the sinking, their numbers were cruelly depleted by shark attacks, saltwater poisoning, hypothermia, and dehydration. When they were finally spotted and rescued, only 317 remained alive. This is their story, recounted by one of their own—Edgar Harrell—a young member of the ship's U.S. Marine detachment. It is an unparalleled account of perseverance, courage, self-sacrifice, and faith.

———

It has been a great blessing to spend most of my life in the company of heroes. By "hero" I mean a person who has wittingly put himself in grave physical jeopardy for the benefit of another. Heroes are people who overcome evil by doing good at great personal risk. Through self-sacrifice, fortitude, and action, whether they succeed or fail, heroes provide a moral and ethical framework—and inspiration—for the rest of us.

Unfortunately, our modern definition of *hero* has been stretched to include all manner of people. The athlete who just set a new sports record isn't a hero. Nor is the "daring" movie star or even the adventurer out to be the first solo climber to scale Mount Everest. They may be brave—but they don't meet the definition of a hero, for whatever they achieve benefits only themselves.

Real heroes are selfless. My father was one. Many of the Marines with whom I was privileged to serve for nearly a quarter of a century were heroes. The firemen and police who rushed into the World Trade Center buildings and the Pentagon on 9/11 fit the description. Today, a good number of young soldiers, sailors, airmen, Marines, and Guardsmen that I cover for FOX News certainly meet the criteria. And Edgar Harrell, survivor of the catastrophic sinking of the USS *Indianapolis*, is a hero.

———————

The true story that Edgar Harrell and his son, David, recount in the pages that follow is far more than a tale of terror on the sea. Together, they have prepared a timely and relevant work for a new generation of Americans once again confronting an enemy that teaches young men not how to live, but how to die the right way. The kamikaze pilot who crashed his plane into the *Indianapolis* on March 31, 1945, differs little from the nineteen terrorists of 9/11 or the suicide car-bombers trying to kill U.S. soldiers and Marines today in the Middle East.

All of that, and much more, is in this book. It is a gripping tale of men tested beyond anything they thought possible—and how they responded with bravery, endurance, and faith in the face of fear and overwhelming despair. Edgar Harrell is not the only hero in this book. But his faith is a testament to the Marine Corps motto: *Semper Fidelis*—Latin for "always faithful."

Lt. Col. Oliver L. North, USMC (Ret.)
Host of *War Stories*
FOX News Channel

Where can I go from Your Spirit?
   Or where can I flee
from Your presence?
If I ascend to heaven, You are there;
If I make my bed in Sheol,
   behold, You are there.
If I take the wings of the dawn,
If I dwell in the remotest part of the sea,
Even there Your hand will lead me,
And Your right hand will lay hold of me.

Psalm 139:7–10

Introduction

by David Harrell

It is easy to grow up in the United States of America and take for granted the wonderful freedom we enjoy. I confess that I have been guilty of being unintentionally indifferent about our nation's liberty, and perhaps even harboring an unwitting apathy concerning the wars that bought it. All too often Memorial Day and Veterans Day come and go with little serious reflection about the enormous sacrifices that have been made. Maybe this describes you as well. However, the bubble of peace and prosperity that once preserved my cavalier attitude was suddenly popped by the terrorist attacks of 9/11. Instantly, all Americans saw with their own eyes what evil looks like, up close and personal. Our false sense of security exploded along with the Twin Towers, the Pentagon, and United Flight 93 in a Pennsylvania field. With shocking abruptness, we were all reminded that freedom is not free—a simple yet profound truth our veterans know all too well.

Because of 9/11, I began to think deeply about our nation's history. Like never before, the stark realities of past wars and

15

the valiant men and women who fought them were thrust into the forefront of my mind. Almost overnight I developed a keen awareness of the evil that plunged us into World War II—the same kind of wickedness that now plagues the world through radical Islam. I also began thinking about the part my father played in that war, along with his shipmates aboard the USS *Indianapolis*.

I remember Dad's reaction to 9/11 was simply, "Here we go again." He was right. The same diabolical evil that motivated our enemies in World War II was once again at work. And once again, men and women of valor must take up arms to ward off barbaric aggressors; heroic soldiers willing to give their lives to preserve our freedom. But what is sad is how quickly we forget the noble military contributions of the past.

I remember hearing Dad talk about the war from time to time when I was a little boy. I recall his reluctant stories about the secret mission of the *Indianapolis*, the atomic bomb components they carried, and especially the gripping tales about the sharks when the crew was lost at sea for five days. I even remember attending some of the *Indianapolis* reunions and meeting Captain McVay and being awestruck by his white Navy uniform and medals. Still, the depth of my father's sacrifice, and that of all the other World War II veterans, did not really hit me until 9/11. I became a man on a mission. Not just to tell my father's story and honor the crew of the USS *Indianapolis*, but to raise the awareness of the cost of freedom and to rekindle the fires of true, God-honoring patriotism and respect for our veterans. Fortunately Dad agreed with my goals, but with even greater passion due to his personal experience.

My father, like many other World War II veterans, has had many opportunities to speak around the country in a variety of venues, including public schools. In interviewing him to write this book, I was saddened to hear about the prevailing ignorance most students have concerning World War II. He indicated that even many of the teachers and administrators he has met admitted they knew little about the war, not to mention the USS *Indianapolis* tragedy. This only fueled my fire to collaborate with my ex-Marine father in educating readers about the heroism of our veterans and ultimately glorifying God.

As you read this harrowing true adventure, you will quickly see the power of faith and the undeniable hand of divine providence in the affairs of men and governments. You will see the crippling effects of sin in the ravages of war and the transforming power of the gospel of Christ in the hearts of men. You will see the corruption of personal revenge and politics, even in our own military, that stooped to tactics of questionable integrity and succumbed to the temptations of injustice. But you will also rejoice in the victory of honor and honesty when a terrible wrong was righted because of the perseverance of those who would never stop fighting for truth. And certainly you will be deeply touched by the valor and humility of sailors and Marines who endured the unimaginable.

Finally, you will learn of a man, like many others, who truly loves his country and his Savior and Lord, Jesus Christ. Without reservation I can say that there is no hypocrisy here. My whole life I have watched my father practice what he has preached. He has been my mentor and friend, and for this I am eternally grateful. Every fiber of his being is dedicated to Christ—validated by his love for my dear mother and all of his family, friends, and his shipmates of the USS *Indianapolis*.

But I must hasten to add, while the steel of his faith was forged in eternity past by a sovereign God, it was undoubtedly tempered in the fires of his adversity at sea. No man could possibly be the same after enduring such a crucible of grace. And it is my prayer, along with my father's, that you too will never be the same after reading this story.

David Harrell

I said to the LORD, "You are my God; give ear,
O LORD, to the voice of my supplications.
O God the LORD, the strength of my salvation,
You have covered my head in the day of battle."

Psalm 140:6–7

CHAPTER

ONE

A Call to Arms

Every survivor of war has stories to tell—stories of triumph and tragedy, faith and fear—stories like mine, where fact is often stranger than fiction. Since that fateful night in 1945 when I stepped off a sinking ship into the unknown depths of the Pacific Ocean, there has never been a day when I have not reflected upon the horrors I experienced in the four and a half days of swimming in shark-infested waters. However, while those frightening memories remain vivid in my mind's eye, one memory eclipses them all—namely, the unfailing presence of God that sustained me.

Luck had absolutely nothing to do with my survival. I believe with all my heart that it was solely by the providence of God that I lived through those dreadful days and nights.

From Turkey Creek to the Marines

I am sure that my background is little different than hundreds of thousands of other folks who grew up in our great country

21

during the Depression and World War II. I suppose we all developed a survivor mind-set in those days of adversity.

I was born in a small house near the banks of the Tennessee River on October 10, 1924, in a little western Kentucky community called Turkey Creek. I was the oldest son of a family of two girls and seven boys. Descendants of the British Isles, we lived on a small farm where my dad was a hard-working farmer, carpenter, and, when necessary, schoolteacher. Mom was our best friend; she had an amazing ability to provide for her family by cooking, sewing, helping in the garden, canning vegetables, and caring for her henhouse, a husband, and nine children.

Those were days of Spartan living. Shoes came once a year from Sears Roebuck, and, for the most part, we made our own toys. Life was simple back then: work or starve! But we were happy. With their faith deeply rooted in the Lord Jesus Christ, my parents did all they knew to raise their children for the glory of God.

My family—like thousands of others across our great nation—had no way of knowing that wicked men across the sea had our great country in their crosshairs. Little did we know that they even considered our safe little Kentucky farm part of a great spoil of war. I'm sure we took our freedom for granted in many ways; after all, freedom was all we had ever known. But by the time I was a junior in high school, the war in the Pacific was in full swing. With the decisive battle at Midway proving to be a turning point for the Allied forces in the Pacific, and convinced that my home and family were in imminent danger, I felt compelled to do my part by volunteering for the United States Marine Corps. In the fall of 1943, when the corn crop was "laid by," I went to the draft board and asked to join the Marines.

I remember well those days of duty and honor. I felt proud I would be serving my country, and even more honored to be able to protect my family and friends. As I listened to our old Silvertone radio, it sounded as though the Japanese were ready to storm the beaches of California. All of those Pacific islands seemed much closer in my limited and naïve comprehension, and I said to myself, "The Japanese must be stopped!"

Years later I discovered that my fear of a Japanese invasion was not as silly as it sounded. The Japanese commander who sunk the USS *Indianapolis* later revealed that one of their submarines actually did launch a small-scale attack on California. In his book *Sunk*, Lt. Cdr. Mochitsura Hashimoto writes,

> On February 24, 1942, submarine *I-17* penetrated the Santa Barbara Straits to the north of Los Angeles, and made the first submarine bombardment of America itself. The boat surfaced five minutes before sunset and fired rapidly at a target indicated by the captain at the periscope. There was evidence of panic on shore. Air-raid sirens were sounded. After firing ten rounds, *I-17* retired at high speed on the surface. En route she met an enemy destroyer hurrying to the scene of action, but slipped by unnoticed.[1]

Even if I had known of this small invasion, I really don't think it would have made much difference to me. This was a fight for freedom, a fight for survival, and a war where evil must be vanquished so justice and freedom could prevail. So, with the soul of a patriot and the heart of a warrior, I committed myself to the Marines. After having been sworn in in Indianapolis, Indiana, I was sent back to my home in Kentucky before reporting for duty.

Joining the service, or even being drafted, was an honorable undertaking in those days. We never heard of protesters, draft

The Harrell family (1940), Turkey Creek, Kentucky. I'm the tallest boy in the back row, on the left side.

dodgers, or flag burners. When the war broke out, patriotism swelled in America. We willingly rationed clothes, food, fuel, and other resources. It seemed that every able-bodied person was involved in working to defend America in some way or another.

On the day I was to report for duty, I remember my dad took me to the bus station and we said our good-byes. Dad was thirty-nine and I was nineteen. Leaving home wasn't easy. Not only was I leaving Mom and Dad, but also two sisters and six brothers. What made it even worse was I also had to leave a certain young lady who had caught my eye one day at school, a girl named Ola Mae Cathey.

Soon I found myself enduring boot camp in San Diego, California. Boot camp was tough and demanding, but I appreciated their commitment to see to it that we were well trained. They knew our lives would depend upon it. When I completed boot camp I was sent to "Sea School" and learned I would be assigned to a large combat ship. Somehow I knew then in my heart that God was up to something in my life far beyond my understanding. Far from the safety of my beloved Kentucky, I found myself alone in a world filled with dangerous unknowns, relieved only by the comforting truth of God's promise, "I will never leave thee, nor forsake thee. . . . The Lord is my helper, and I will not fear what man shall do unto me" (Hebrews 13:5–6 KJV). In March 1944 I was assigned to the USS *Indianapolis*, and this was to be my home until her sinking on July 30, 1945.

The USS *Indianapolis* (CA-35)

I still remember my first impression when I boarded the *Indy*, as she was affectionately called: *This thing is big—really big!* It was like a floating city. For a country boy from Kentucky, it was overwhelming. The sight of the massive guns gave me goose bumps. Never having seen guns larger than a double-barreled shotgun, I remember laughing to myself, thinking, *My, my, my. We can win the war just by ourselves with these monsters!*

By many accounts, the *Indianapolis* was the pride of the U.S. Navy. Built for speed, her keel (the structural part under the hull) was laid down in Camden, New Jersey, on March 31, 1930, by the New York Shipbuilding Corp., and she was launched on November 7, 1931. After being properly outfitted for military service, she was officially commissioned by the Navy in the Philadelphia Navy Yard on November 15, 1932.

She was enormous at 610 feet, 3 inches long, and 66 feet 1 inch at her widest point. Her keel lay 24 feet below the surface

> The *Indianapolis* was the largest ship I had ever seen. Having grown up during the Depression in Chicago, seeing the magnificent ship was one of the greatest moments of my life. I hadn't seen a boat much bigger than a canoe for most of my life—the biggest thing I had ever seen was a barge offshore on Lake Michigan. Not only was the *Indianapolis* larger than this barge, but I got to see it sitting right there in the bay before me.
>
> Survivor Michael N. Kuryla Jr.

when she was fully loaded with men, arms, and provisions. Armed with the latest technology of her day and loaded with four Parsons turbines that gave her a total of 107,000 horsepower, she was designed to travel at a maximum speed of 32 knots (over 36 mph).

I was fascinated to learn that the *Indianapolis* had been chosen by President Roosevelt as his Ship of State. Her speed and massive firepower truly captured the spirit of America. Before the war, Roosevelt used her on numerous occasions to entertain royalty and great leaders from around the world as she frequently crossed the Atlantic and toured the great ports of South America.

She was armed with three turrets—two fore and one aft—each containing three 8-inch guns. She also had four 5-inch guns and twenty-four intermediate-range 40 mm guns, of which both types I learned to operate. And in several overhauls during the war, thirty-two 20 mm Oerlikon guns were added.[2]

From the start, I was determined to make the best of my new home. The bunks (or sleeping racks) were stacked three high,

Proud to be a United States Marine (1945).

and of course new recruits got the top ones, so my sleeping quarters were small and hot. They sure were a far cry from the feather bed I had at home. But why complain, and who would I even complain to? That said, I must admit that I shed many a tear those lonely, homesick days and nights. I often poured out my heart to the Lord as I faced the unknowns of the future.

Now, as a Marine having been joined to a detachment of thirty-nine Marine officers and enlisted men, I knew that I had a job to do and a load to carry. It would be our job to manage the ship's brig (guardhouse) and operate various weapon systems, but also lead any potential landing operations that might be required. It was an honor to be part of the ship's company of the *Indianapolis* that would eventually earn ten battle stars.

A Mysterious Departure

Years after the war I learned of some intriguing history involving the *Indianapolis* that helps set the stage for the story you are about to read. In April 1940, when tensions concerning Japanese aggression began to mount, the U.S. Fleet, including the *Indianapolis*, was moved from the West Coast to Pearl Harbor, Hawaii. But just before the Japanese attack at Pearl Harbor, the *Indianapolis* was suspiciously removed from port, as if someone knew what was coming and wanted to protect her. To this day, these unexplained maneuverings remain a mystery. One historian writes:

> Officially, on the day the Japanese struck Pearl Harbor, December 7th, 1941, the *Indianapolis* was conveniently out of her home port, Pearl Harbor, making a simulated bombardment of Johnson Island off to the west. Captain E. W. Hanson, USN, was then in command. It is noteworthy to mention here that all of the carriers assigned to Pearl were also conveniently out of Pearl as well. *Indianapolis* immediately joined Task Force 12 to search for the attacking Japanese carrier force. Returning to Pearl Harbor, the *Indianapolis* was assigned to Task Force 11 for operations against the enemy.[3]

We may never know with certainty the political and military machinations behind the scenes that resulted in the *Indy*'s orders to leave Pearl Harbor just prior to the Japanese strike. Some have concluded that this is yet another piece of evidence validating the hypothesis that the American forces had prior knowledge of the attack. Certainly the implications are staggering given the loss of life that could possibly have been averted that day.

Daniel E. Brady, seaman second class of the V (Aviation) Division, was on board the *Indianapolis* at the time; a paraphrase of his account of the events follows.

On December 5, 1941, a Friday, they were docked in Pearl Harbor at the mine dock next to the submarine base, across from what was referred to as Battleship Row. That afternoon all the married men and "liberty sections" (men who were given authorized absence) were ashore, which was the normal routine while they were at port on weekends. That left about one-third of the crew on board and on duty. Suddenly, word was passed that the ship would be getting underway in only an hour, an impossible task. Brady shared:

> Most of our crew were ashore and we could never recall them in time on such short notice. Soon, fifty Marines in full battle gear came aboard, followed by forty or so civilian shipyard workers with their toolboxes. Next came truckloads of food and vegetables, which were dumped unceremoniously on the bleached, white, teakwood quarterdeck!

The quarterdeck, which is part of a ship's upper deck near the stern, is generally set apart for admirals, captains, and other official and ceremonial usage. Tossing food onto its surface would have been unheard of. In fact, enlisted men weren't even allowed to walk across it with their shoes on.

Sure enough, the *Indianapolis* was underway in one hour's time, leaving behind much of her crew as she steamed out of Pearl Harbor. The crew on board was not told where they were headed until they arrived Sunday morning at a small island about seven hundred miles southwest of Hawaii. As the crew began unloading, they heard rumblings and rumors that the Japanese were bombing Pearl Harbor. Immediately they had to prepare the ship for battle.

They threw overboard everything that had the potential to burn, from lumber and small boats to President Roosevelt's

The USS *Indianapolis* (CA-35), 1945, in the last known photograph of the great ship, just days before she was sunk. (Bureau of Ships Collection, U.S. National Archives)

own beautiful bedroom suite that he used when he was aboard (since the *Indianapolis* was his favorite ship). Then the *Indianapolis* sailed for Hawaiian waters once again and joined up with the *Lexington*, an aircraft carrier. But they weren't able to enter Pearl Harbor for seven days—attempting three times—as Japanese submarines were trying to sink the *Lexington* in the entrance to the harbor.

Finally they made it into the harbor and looked upon the damage that the attack had wrought. If they had remained there, the *Indianapolis* would have surely been destroyed. Brady, among others, believed someone must have known the attack would take place and made sure it sailed away to safety at just the right time. Whether they're right, I cannot say.[4]

In some ways it seems as though I never left the *Indy*. Indeed, her story lives on even after all these years, even though—or because of—the mystery that shrouds her story. Perhaps no other ship in wartime history has grabbed the interest of the American people like the *Indianapolis*. To her crew she was the queen of the fleet. Spared at Pearl Harbor, yet sacrificed for the cause at the deciding climax of WWII, the USS *Indianapolis* gave her all. As you will see, her fate stretches the limits of bad luck to the breaking point. There was something far greater at work, something supernatural, a force that orchestrated her every move.

To every thing there is a season, and a
time to every purpose under the heaven:
A time to be born, and a time to die;
a time to plant, and a time to pluck
    up that which is planted;
A time to kill, and a time to heal;
a time to break down, and a time to build up;
A time to weep, and a time to laugh;
a time to mourn, and a time to dance . . .
A time to love, and a time to hate;
a time of war, and a time of peace.

Ecclesiastes 3:1–4, 8 KJV

TWO

The *Indy Maru*

While the war raged across the sea, the USS *Indianapolis* was being refitted with more sophisticated radar and gunnery equipment at Mare Island, San Francisco. My first duties as a Marine were on what we called Goat Island in the San Francisco area, guarding Navy and Marine personnel confined to the brig. Several weeks passed before I had received my orders to board the USS *Indianapolis*, affectionately nicknamed the *Indy Maru*. Most ships were given nicknames, and though it is not known how the *Indianapolis* got hers, it is interesting to note that *maru* is the Japanese word for "ship."[1]

I'll never forget that exhilarating day we first sailed out of Mare Island in the early part of 1944. The reality that I was off to war really began to sink in. I could not possibly be aware of the demonstration of divine providence that would see me through it all.

I was naïvely excited as our skipper, Capt. E. R. Johnson, set course for our first destination: Pearl Harbor. There we were to "pick up our flag"—Navy talk for picking up an admiral, ours being Adm. Raymond A. Spruance, commander of the Fifth Fleet. I can still remember the first time I saw Admiral Spruance walking on the forward deck of the *Indianapolis*. He would do it often, and for long periods of time almost every day. I can only imagine the stress he had to endure given the enormity of his responsibilities. He was an impressive man who easily earned respect. He gave his young sailors and Marines confidence as we prepared for battle. We were all proud to serve under him.

Combat Aboard Ship

My first combat experience was at Kwajalein and Eniwetok in the Marshall Island chain (see map in chapter 7). That action was primarily a clean-up operation, destroying any remaining installations through heavy bombardment. Our ultimate sights, however, were on Guam, Saipan, and Tinian, crucial islands for providing a staging area for our new Boeing B-29 Superfortress bombers to be able to attack the mainland of Japan.

From the Marshalls we moved on to attack the Western Carolines to soften them up for our Marines to land. There our carrier planes struck the enemy at the Palau Islands and bombed enemy airfields, sinking three destroyers, seventeen freighters, and five oilers, and damaging another seventeen enemy ships. We shot 160 Japanese planes out of the sky during these air strikes, and destroyed another forty-six on the ground.[2]

Fighting aboard the *Indy* was exhausting at times. Many times the Japanese would be firing at us from their island fortifications as we returned fire with our big guns. At the same time, I would be firing my 40 mm guns at their aircraft buzzing overhead to prevent them from hitting us. In my peripheral vision I could see water splashing, planes falling, and smoke rising from some of our ships that had been hit. I remember thinking, *This can't be happening. Am I really here?* The noise was deafening and I was terrified, running on pure adrenalin.

In the Western Carolines we manned our guns for seventeen days straight in an effort to destroy the tremendous concrete tunnels and fortifications the Japanese had so effectively built. Tragically, our American forces lost approximately seven thousand men during the months of March and April of 1944 at Yap, Ulithi, Woleai, and Palau. Although loss of life was high, these were strategic victories because they neutralized the enemy's ability to interfere with the U.S. landings on New Guinea (though some argued we would have been better off to have starved them out than gone in after them).

On June 13, we moved on to the Marianas, where the *Indianapolis* joined the pre-invasion bombardment group off Saipan. The Japanese were dug in deep on Saipan with their massive gun installations camouflaged and concealed behind trapdoors on concrete bunkers. With the landing attack scheduled for June 15, Admiral Spruance maneuvered the *Indianapolis* close enough to oversee the attack—so close, in fact, that we experienced many near misses from the Japanese batteries. Fortunately, we were hit only one time by a defective shell that did not explode, causing only minor damage.

Under the cover of ferocious American bombardment, the Second and Third Marine divisions launched their amphibious assault, but they were met with stiff resistance when they came ashore. The well-fortified Japanese bunkers were high above the beaches, capable of quickly opening their massive trapdoors to blast our vulnerable boys below before concealing

The USS *Indianapolis* under fire by Japanese shore batteries during the invasion of Saipan, June 1944. (U.S. Naval Historical Center)

themselves again. The casualties for our Marines were high. I experienced an almost overwhelming range of emotions that day, everything from fear to fury. Still, not letting our emotions rule us, the crew of the *Indy* fought on with great discipline, doing all we could to support our vulnerable troops storming the beaches.

Desperate to relieve their beleaguered forces to the south in the Marianas, the Japanese launched a large fleet of battleships, carriers, cruisers, and destroyers. According to Tokyo Rose (a generic term for English-speaking Japanese broadcasters that spread propaganda over the airwaves), the Americans were running away from the massive flotilla of the Japanese Navy. To the contrary, Admiral Spruance ordered a fast carrier force to make haste to meet them head on. A second force attacked their air bases at Iwo Jima and Chichi Jima in the Bonin and Volcano Islands. Admiral Spruance was confident of victory knowing that the United States had 104 ships of various kinds and 819 carrier-based planes available in the theater of operation. Estimates for the Japanese, however, indicated that they had suffered serious losses in the Pacific, leaving them with only 55 ships and 430 planes. By then, the U.S. Fleet had twice as many destroyers as the Japanese.

Our fleet met the enemy on June 19 in what was called the Battle of the Philippine Sea, but became known throughout the fleet as the Marianas Turkey Shoot. According to the Navy Department's Naval History Division, enemy carrier planes had hoped to refuel and rearm at the Guam and Tinian airfields and attack our offshore ships. Instead, they were met by our own carrier planes and the guns of the escorting ships. That day, 402 enemy planes were destroyed while we lost only 17 of our own. In addition to the enemy planes, U.S. carrier planes also managed to sink two enemy carriers, two destroyers, and one tanker, and severely damaged several other ships. The *Indianapolis* triumphantly shot down a torpedo plane.[3]

Kamikaze Planes and the Insanity of War

As Japan's war machine began to fall apart, their desperation gave birth to the concept of suicide planes called *kamikazes*, meaning "divine wind." With their planes loaded with explosives and only enough fuel to make it to their designated target, kamikaze pilots would ceremonially step into their cockpits for the last time, with feelings of great pride, and fly off to their death.

Whenever I reflect on these battles, especially the Marianas Turkey Shoot, I find myself shaking my head at the insanity of war. The suicide missions of the Japanese kamikaze pilots serve as a perfect illustration. What a colossal waste of lives and resources—and for what? Most of the Japanese soldiers, especially the officers, considered their emperor a god and worshiped him. They considered it an honor to die for him. Likewise, most Japanese considered themselves Shintoists (belonging to the religion of Shintoism, primarily a mystical religious system of nature and ancestor worship). This belief system was so powerful that it inspired their soldiers to make *banzai* (fierce and reckless) suicide attacks as an act of religious service. Capture was considered a profound disgrace upon their families, who considered those captured as dead. For this reason Japanese soldiers would rather die than be taken prisoner by the enemy. With such fanaticism, one can only imagine the staggering loss of life if we had been forced to invade Japan with ground forces before they surrendered.

I remember feeling pity for the ones we shot down and rescued. Most were poorly trained young pilots, blinded by a warped sense of patriotism, honor, and, like all suicide warriors, a fanatical religious fervor to serve some phantom god (or gods) that does not exist. I was intrigued as I watched the survivors being lifted out of the sea and placed onto the deck of the *Indy*. Wounded and scared, I can still see their white pajama-like death uniforms and their young faces overwhelmed with terror and confusion. After dressing their wounds and conducting the customary interrogations, we would transfer them to other ships as prisoners of war.

After the Marianas Turkey Shoot, the *Indianapolis* returned to Saipan to resume fire support for six days. We then moved

The *Indy*'s antiaircraft guns firing at a kamikaze plane (1945).

on to Tinian to blast shore installations. Meanwhile, Guam had been taken, and the *Indianapolis* was the first ship to enter Apra Harbor (previously an American base) since the harbor's capture by the Japanese early in the war.

For the next few weeks we operated in the Marianas area and then proceeded back to the Western Carolines, where further landing assaults were planned. From September 12 through 29, both before and after our landings, we bombarded the Island of Peleliu in the Palau Group. We then went on to operate for ten days around the island of Manus in the Admiralty Islands before returning back to San Francisco to the Mare Island Navy Yard for repairs and maintenance.[4]

New Skipper Comes Aboard

In December 1944 we welcomed our new skipper, Capt. Charles B. McVay III. Unlike Captain Johnson, who was all business in his military demeanor, Captain McVay was more personable and enjoyed interacting with the men. Johnson ran a very tight ship, requiring many drills and calling General Quarters (i.e., being battle ready) early in the morning. McVay, on the other hand, ran a looser ship, not requiring us to be battle ready all the time. This means he didn't expect us to keep watertight doors closed and dogged (fastened shut) when we were in forward areas. But I never thought of him as being lax in any way.

I served as a Marine orderly for both of these fine captains and had a bit of a firsthand experience with both of them. I still laugh as I recall driving Captain Johnson down to the Navy Yard one sunny day. He was just as much in charge of that jeep as he was the *Indy*, except on that occasion I was at the controls and the fine captain was in the back seat telling me how to drive.

With Captain McVay now at the helm of the *Indy* and our overhaul at Mare Island complete, we joined Vice Adm. Marc Mitscher's carrier task force on February 14, 1945. There we played a vital support role as our forces attacked the installations in the Home Islands of Japan itself. The *Indy* gave its support to the first air strikes on Tokyo since General Doolittle's invasion in April 1942, preparing the way for the bloody struggles at the landings on Iwo Jima—one of Japan's southernmost islands.[5]

The campaign around the Home Islands stands out in my mind. It was crucial for us to gain tactical surprise, and we did so by traversing the Aleutian Island chain in terrible weather. I remember several occasions where I was at watch on the bridge during high seas. As the ship forged ahead, the bow would descend into the great valleys of water, then plow into the frigid banks of the oncoming waves, causing a sleet-like spray to strike me with stinging force.

Our mission was successful in the Home Islands campaign. Between February 14 and February 17, the Navy lost forty-nine carrier planes while shooting down or destroying 499 enemy planes. Our task force sank one Japanese carrier, nine coastal ships, two destroyer escorts, and a cargo ship. While this was going on, Japan was being systematically devastated every day by our Air Force.[6]

Iwo Jima

With their homeland under attack and their war machine gradually being diminished, the Japanese fought with a zealous determination. They fiercely defended Iwo Jima, proving to be one of the toughest of all the islands for the United States to secure. An estimated 21,000 Japanese troops inhabited the labyrinth of coral tunnels on the volcanic island. The *Indy*'s mission was simple: Bombard them! We had the ability to fire over five hundred rounds of 5-inch gun ammunition in under six minutes, sending massive amounts of destructive flak as far as eight miles. The big 8-inch guns could lob 250-pound shells up to eighteen miles. The concussion from the 8-inchers was staggering. In fact, their enormous recoil would actually move the massive *Indianapolis* sideways in the water. We were also well equipped for close-range warfare with the firepower of our 40 mm and 20 mm deck guns. They were especially effective on kamikaze planes, which were a persistent threat.

I will never forget the day a kamikaze plane flew in low and horizontal, trying to make its way across our bow. As always, our mission was to shoot him before he could get to us. That particular day I was a fuse-box loader on one of the 5-inch guns. I would place a seventy-five-pound shell into a fuse box hitched up to what was called "sky aft radar." This radar system would then relay the actual coordinates of the incoming enemy plane to the shell itself, instructing it to explode its flak precisely in front of the plane.

As the plane came roaring by from left to right, the 5-inch gun immediately to the left of my gun continued firing in its left-to-right range of motion until its rotation was complete. With its muzzle now approximately sixteen feet from where I stood, pointed as far forward as possible toward the bow of the ship, it fired again. The concussion of the blast was so powerful that it knocked me to the deck while I was still holding the seventy-five-pound shell. The explosion dislodged my cotton earplugs, causing them to fall out and quickly blow away in the Pacific wind. Though I was dazed, God enabled me to get to my feet and load the shell. As it fired, the percussion of the blasts further damaged my unprotected ears, causing temporary deafness and blood to run out of my left ear. While our efforts averted the enemy plane and our lives were spared, I permanently suffered a 50 percent loss of hearing in that ear.

Okinawa

By March 4, 1945, we joined the pre-invasion bombardment of Okinawa, where we fired 8-inch shells onto the Japanese beach defenses. In the seven days of fighting at Okinawa, the crew of the *Indy* shot down six planes and assisted in splashing two others.

One morning, the ship's lookouts spotted a single-engine Japanese kamikaze fighter plane diving toward the ship's bridge. We immediately opened fire with our 20 mm guns, and although we hit the plane and caused it to swerve, the pilot was still able to release his bomb, then crashed his plane on the port side of the after main deck of the *Indy*. The plane toppled off the ship and fell into the sea, causing little damage to the surface of the ship, but the bomb tore through the deck armor, the mess hall, the berthing compartment below, and the fuel tanks in the lowest chambers before crashing through the bottom of the ship and exploding in the water underneath us. It was a miracle that we suffered only moderate damage.

The official naval report indicated,

> The concussion blew two gaping holes in the ship bottom and flooded compartments in the area, killing nine crewmen. Although the *Indianapolis* settled slightly by the stern and listed to port, there was no progressive flooding; and the plucky cruiser steamed to a salvage ship for emergency repairs. Here, inspection revealed that her propeller shafts were damaged, her fuel tanks ruptured, her water-distilling equipment ruined; nevertheless, the battle-proud cruiser made the long trip across the Pacific to the Mare Island Navy Yard under her own power.[7]

Top-Secret Cargo

It was a relief to come back to Mare Island and leave the Pacific front. The break from combat was welcomed, but it was short lived. While at Hunters Point in San Francisco, we suddenly received word that all leaves were cancelled. Despite the

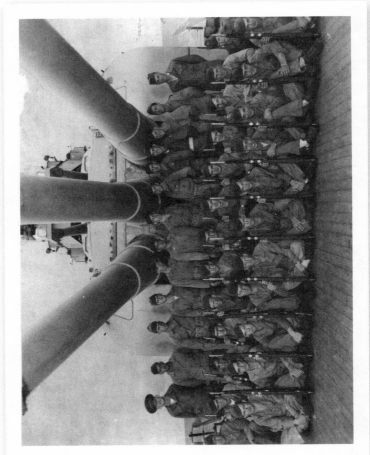

The USS *Indianapolis* Marine Guard under number 1 turret. I am directly under the middle barrel, middle row (1945).

Signatures of most of my fellow Marines, on back of our photo under number 1 turret.

fact that the *Indy* was not fully repaired and tested, we were ordered to get underway immediately. Not knowing what was going on, we boarded and quickly followed orders as we loaded last-minute provisions.

There was an obvious tension in the air—a mood of excitement combined with confusion and secrecy. The place was crawling with Marine guards and top military brass. My curiosity was fueled even more when I was ordered to station guards around the mysterious cargo that had been brought aboard. A large crate, measuring about five feet high, five feet wide, and perhaps fifteen feet in length, was hoisted onto the port hangar off the quarterdeck—an area normally used to store, catapult, and retrieve small observation airplanes.

The plywood crate had been latched onto the deck with large straps fastened by countersunk screws. Each countersunk void was filled with a red-wax seal to serve as a tamper indicator. After stationing guards around the mysterious container, I was given orders to do the same for another curious piece of cargo brought aboard that was placed in a compartment on the upper deck, which was reserved strictly for officers.

> As we entered the cabin, three men were already there. We saw two lead canisters, about knee-high, with long steel pipes through rings on top. As I made my way to the opposite side, I said, "This looks like it has to do with radiation." Silence . . . The two escorts, later identified as Captain Nolan and Major Furman, looked at each other but said nothing.
>
> Survivor Richard A. Paroubek

There I stationed a guard outside one of Admiral Spruance's unused rooms, since he was not on board at the time. Inside the room was an ominous-looking black metal canister that a couple of sailors had brought on board. The canister was about two feet long and maybe eighteen inches wide, and was padlocked in a steel cage that had been welded securely to the deck floor. A new boarder to the ship by the name of Captain Nolan had the key to the padlock. Adding to the suspense, the crew was warned that whatever happened in the days to come, *that canister must not be lost or destroyed.* Whatever it contained was obviously of enormous importance. I later discovered that when the black canister was aboard the transport plane, it had its very own parachute, just in case something went wrong.

Captain Nolan and another Army officer who boarded the ship with him, Maj. Robert Furman, remained with the secret cargo. They seemed conspicuously nervous and out of place, and stayed to themselves in the days that followed. Weeks later we discovered that they were not military officers at all, but rather two scientists in disguise from the top-secret weapons labs in Los Alamos, New Mexico. And the cargo? Integral components of the atomic bombs that would be dropped three weeks later on Hiroshima and Nagasaki, code named "Little Boy" and "Fat Man."

The ominous canister contained uranium-235; it accounted for approximately half the fissionable material possessed by the United States, and it was valued around $300 million. According to one historian, "The contents of the crate were known to only a handful of people: President Truman and Winston Churchill; Robert Oppenheimer and his closest colleagues at the Manhattan Project; and Captain James Nolan and Major

Robert Furman, who were now aboard the *Indy*. In reality, Nolan was a radiologist and Furman an engineer engaged in top-secret weapons intelligence."[8]

Full Speed Ahead—a Record Run

On July 16, 1945, at 8:30 a.m., we exited San Francisco Bay and set sail for Pearl Harbor, Hawaii. Being one of the fastest ships in the Navy, the *Indianapolis* made record time, covering 2,405 miles in just over seventy-four hours. Taking just six hours to load up on supplies and fuel, we left Pearl Harbor and immediately sailed unescorted to the island of Tinian, arriving there on July 26. In total, the *Indianapolis* had set a record of some 5,300 miles covering San Francisco to our B-29 base in Tinian in only ten days.[9]

Tinian Island, a small island along the Marianas Trench, is approximately twelve miles in length and six miles in width. At just one hundred nautical miles north of Guam, its proximity to Japan made it a strategic B-29 Superfortress airbase. The four runways of the north field were extended to a length of 8,500 feet to accommodate gigantic aircraft burdened with heavy bombs and extra fuel needed to complete nightly twelve-hour round-trip raids on Japan.

Although our bombing raids were having a devastating impact on the enemy, Washington had made plans to invade Japan with two operations involving over two million American soldiers. Under the code name "Olympic," 800,000 troops were to go ashore on the southern island of Kyushu in November, with a second amphibious assault called "Coronet" to land on the island of Honshu near Tokyo in April 1946.

None of us aboard the *Indianapolis* had any idea that the mysterious cargo we had just unloaded at Tinian would make all these plans unnecessary. None of us knew that we had just delivered the most devastating weapon in the history of the world. None of us knew that God was using the crew of the *Indianapolis* to accomplish His purposes in bringing the war to an abrupt and terrifying end. And certainly none of us knew that four days after arriving in Tinian, our beloved *Indy Maru* and most of her crew would be lost at sea.

Those who go down to the sea in ships,
who do business on great waters;
They have seen the works of the LORD,
and His wonders in the deep.
For He spoke and raised up a stormy wind,
which lifted up the waves of the sea.

They rose up to the heavens, they
went down to the depths;
Their soul melted away in their misery.
They reeled and staggered like a drunken man,
and were at their wits' end.

Then they cried to the LORD in their trouble,
and He brought them out of their distresses.
He caused the storm to be still, so that
the waves of the sea were hushed.
Then they were glad because they were quiet,
So He guided them to their desired haven.

Let them give thanks to the LORD
for His lovingkindness,
And for His wonders to the sons of men!
Let them extol Him also in the
congregation of the people,
And praise Him at the seat of the elders.

Psalm 107:23–32

 CHAPTER

THREE

Tragedy Explodes—
the First Day

You never know what a new day will bring. As a Christian, I have learned that even my most carefully made plans are ultimately subservient to the will of God; our plans are not our own. With our top-secret cargo now safely delivered to the B-29 base at Tinian, we were ordered to proceed the hundred or so miles south to Guam, and later to sail on to Leyte to meet up with the battleship USS *Idaho* for seventeen days of drills. There we would be familiarized with new equipment and conduct gunnery practice with a partially new crew in need of training. We would also get prepared to participate in the invasion of Kyushu, one of Japan's southernmost islands. Overall, this journey was a dangerous 1,300-mile jaunt that would take us out of the relatively safe Marianas Sea Frontier and into the vast unknowns of the Philippine Sea Frontier. Little did we know the horrors that awaited us.

Since the *Indy* had no sonar gear to detect enemy submarines—a task relegated to destroyers—it was revealed later that
Captain McVay had asked for a destroyer escort for added protection. His request was denied. The command center for the
Pacific, known as CINCPAC, insisted the waters were safe.[1]

To hide the United States' ability to decipher encrypted Japanese command messages through an ingenious top-secret code-
breaking program called ULTRA, the U.S. command maintained
a policy to randomly withhold precise enemy ship locations
from Navy captains. This allowed some Japanese ships to avoid
being attacked, giving them the impression that we had not
broken their code and thereby avoiding the possibility of them
changing their encryption codes and making our deciphering
system obsolete.[2]

In light of this policy, CINCPAC intelligence did not inform
Captain McVay that the Japanese Tamon submarine group had
been patrolling our anticipated route. They also did not report
that just days earlier, a destroyer escort, the USS *Underhill*, had
been sunk by a kaiten released from a large Japanese patrol sub
on the same route we would be navigating to Leyte.[3] A kaiten
(literally, "the turn toward heaven") is a manned suicide torpedo.
The mentality of their pilots was naturally very similar to that of
kamikaze pilots. Each kaiten required a two-man crew, weighed
about eight tons, and contained powerful explosive warheads.
Their estimated top speed was about 20 knots (23 mph), and
they were capable of traveling up to twenty-seven miles. Fanatical kaiten pilots were always ready to climb inside and steer
themselves into glory—unless they missed, as was often the case.
Since the kaitens were not recoverable, they would simply run
out of fuel and silently sink to the ocean floor where both man
and machine would be crushed by the enormous water pressure.

A Japanese kaiten; the human torpedo.

Traversing the Unknown

Unescorted and uninformed, the *Indy* arrived in Guam on July 27 and from there headed to the Leyte Gulf. Life aboard ship was relaxed for the crew as we went about our daily operations. Of course we knew nothing of the skipper's concerns about our vulnerability.

The temperature was a tropical 110 degrees during the day— hot and muggy. Although air was pumped into our cramped chambers below deck, it still felt like a sauna, making it almost impossible for any of us to sleep at night. The temperature in the engine rooms usually exceeded 120 degrees, even with all the hatches and doors open to draw in any outside breeze. For this reason we were given permission to sleep topside on the open deck. Each of us found our own open space to spread out our blankets so we could enjoy our designated four hours of sleep.

We were traveling in "Yoke-Modified" position, which is a more relaxed state of sailing that is normal for waters perceived to be safe from enemy attack. Our battle-ready state, "Condition Able," meant that we were on watch for four hours, then off for four hours—an exhausting schedule that left little time for rest. Had we known of the danger that lay ahead, we would have traveled at the most secure position, with all hatches and doors dogged and sealed off, making passage very limited, a position known as "Zed."[4]

It is only human to reflect on that fateful night and play the "What if . . ." game. Certainly there was a high probability that things would have turned out much differently had we been properly informed and prepared. But it's history now; everything unfolded according to God's intended plan and for His purposes.

We were traveling according to the fallacious conditions and instructions outlined for us at CINCPAC—good reason for the ultimate blame for the ensuing tragedy to have been placed on the high command of the Navy.

On the night of July 29, the sea was relatively calm with overcast skies. Captain McVay agreed to cease the presumably defensive zigzag maneuver thought to create a more evasive target—a naval regulation later proven to be ineffective. Lieutenant McKissick took the watch on the bridge at 6:00 p.m.[5] The ship was on course 262 True, which was due west. Noting the overcast skies, Captain McVay entered the bridge and said to McKissick, "You may secure from zigzagging after twilight." McKissick responded, "Aye, aye, sir." And steadily the *Indy* continued on to her destiny.[6]

I got off watch around midnight and decided to grab my blanket from my locker below and sleep topside on the breezy deck. The night before, I stretched the regulations a bit and slept on top of number 1 turret in a large life raft. A Marine buddy by the name of Munson had the same idea and joined me there. But on this night, not wanting to risk losing any of my hard-earned stripes (having made Sergeant just two days before), I chose instead to sleep on the open deck under the barrels of number 1 turret.

The *Indy* was cruising at about seventeen knots. Her large engines, combined with the sound of her wake, droned a familiar lullaby. Tired and homesick, and missing my family and my little brunette back home, I wrapped my blanket around me and curled up on the steel deck hoping for a few hours of rest. After thanking the Lord for His provision and protection thus far, I asked Him to watch over my loved ones back in Kentucky. Then, using the arch of my shoe for a pillow, I drifted off to sleep.

Enemy in Wait

While I had innocently fallen asleep in harm's way, I and everyone else aboard the *Indy* were utterly unaware that the Japanese submarine *I-58*, under the command of Lt. Cdr. Mochitsura Hashimoto, had been silently slithering through the dark sea with its serpentine periscope and had spotted us at about midnight.

The *I-58* was a formidable submarine measuring 356 feet in length. Although the normal safe diving depth for Japanese submarines was 300 feet, the *I-58* was designed to go even deeper to evade its enemies, capable of descending to 450 feet.[7] It had been commissioned in September 1944 and carried a crew of 105 officers and men.[8]

It was part of the celebrated Tamon group—one of six submarines left in the dwindling Japanese fleet. She was powered by two 4,700-horsepower diesel engines capable of gliding through the water at seventeen knots and could travel 21,000 miles before refueling. Commander Hashimoto had in his arsenal

nineteen torpedoes and six kaitens, complete with twelve suicide warriors.[9]

The *I-58* had just been fitted with two new kinds of radar
equipment, one for detecting surface ships and one for detecting aircraft. The sub was also well equipped with both
electronic and acoustic sonar. Since they were armed with
kaitens, the open deck had been stripped to only one 25 mm
machine gun.[10]

Commander Hashimoto had been at sea for four years and
had yet to destroy an enemy ship. He was desperate for a kill.
Now he had his chance. The noble *Indianapolis* was an easy
target as she unwittingly made her way into the crosshairs of
Hashimoto's periscope. According to the testimony of Hashimoto given many months later, no kaitens were needed—a dis-
appointment for the crewmembers who wanted to be launched.
The exhilaration of a possible "first kill" combined with the
anxiety of engaging the enemy caused tension to run high aboard
the *I-58*. In his book *Sunk*, Commander Hashimoto describes
what happened after his navigator shouted, "Bearing red nine-
zero degrees, a possible enemy ship!"[11]

At 12:08 a.m., when the *I-58* was fully submerged, Commander Hashimoto gave three orders: "Ship in sight," "All tubes
to the ready," and "Kaitens stand by." After the submarine dove,
it altered course to port so that the black shape that was the USS
Indianapolis was straight ahead. Hashimoto was still unsure
of what it was, but it seemed to be getting closer as it took a
course directly toward the submarine. He was ready to launch
six torpedoes, but at this point he still thought it might have
been a destroyer that had already detected the submarine and
was approaching for a depth-charge attack. (It was impossible
at that time to determine how far away a ship was unless you

Japanese Lt. Cdr. Mochitsura Hashimoto at the periscope of his submarine, the *I-58*.
(Edgar Harrell Collection)

knew the class—and therefore the size—of the ship.) Even if it wasn't a destroyer, he couldn't let us get directly overhead or we wouldn't be in good position for a torpedo hit.

Hashimoto watched the black shadow of the *Indy* grow slowly into a triangular shape, clarifying the distance and positioning. At 12:09 he announced, "Six torpedoes will be fired," choosing to fire from all tubes in a single salvo. He also ordered one of the kaiten crews to enter their craft and another to stand by.

The *Indianapolis* was now becoming more visible from Hashimoto's point of view; he could tell that we were either a battleship or a large cruiser, and he was able to assess the masthead height as ninety feet. He felt confident he'd be able to hit his

The Japanese submarine *I-58*. (U.S. Marine Corps)

target, as we were now four thousand yards away and sailing toward the *I-58* at a moderately high speed.

As Hashimoto was setting his torpedoes, he still hadn't given the kaitens their orders to launch. The phase of the moon was not ideal for a kaiten attack, as they could be seen and destroyed before hitting their mark, so Hashimoto decided not to launch them unless the ordinary torpedoes failed. The *Indy* was now clearly visible in the moonlight. Hashimoto saw the two turrets aft and the large tower mast and incorrectly took her to be an Idaho-class battleship. Dead quiet now, they waited. Hashimoto altered the setting to "green sixty degrees" and a range of fifteen hundred yards.

At long last, he gave the order: "Stand by—fire!" Soon the report came from the torpedo room that all tubes had been fired. Hashimoto watched through his periscope, waiting as six torpedoes sped toward the *Indianapolis*. He ordered the submarine to be brought parallel to the enemy ship. Finally, a column of water shot up on the *Indy*'s starboard side by the forward turret, and then another by the aft turret. Immediately red flames shot out of the ship, and then another huge column of water that seemed to engulf the entire ship rose from the area by number 2 turret. Hashimoto shouted, "A hit! A hit!" and his crew danced for joy.

Soon came the sound of a heavy explosion, much louder than the torpedo hits themselves. Three more explosions followed, then another six. The crew of the submarine mistakenly thought it was a depth charge attack and briefly panicked, but Hashimoto assured them there were no other ships in sight—it was just the enemy ship exploding. Several more flashes came from the *Indy*, but still she didn't sink. Hashimoto planned to give a second salvo of torpedoes even though the kaiten pilots asked to be sent to finish the job. Their job seemed easy enough now, despite the moonlight, but he knew that once they were launched they could not be retrieved. He didn't want to waste them if it was unnecessary.

As soon as they reloaded the torpedoes, the *I-58* resurfaced and raised the periscope. But there was now nothing to be seen. Hashimoto ordered them to head for the area in which the *Indy* had sunk, but there was still no trace of the "enemy" ship. Nevertheless, he was certain that a ship that had been as damaged as the *Indy* had could not have escaped. And even if she'd stayed afloat, she would have still been in sight—there was no way she could have gotten away that quickly. Nevertheless, Hashimoto later admitted he wished he had proof. Fearing reprisals from any ships or aircraft that might have been accompanying the *Indy*, he made off to the northeast. After staying on the surface for an hour, they dove and prepared for their next encounter.[12]

The Front of the Ship . . . Was Gone

There has not been a season in my life since that night that I
fail to remember what happened next. The first torpedo pierced
the *Indy* on the forward starboard side about forty feet in front
of number 1 turret, where I slept. The concussion jarred me
instantly to my feet. In the time it took Commander Hashimoto
to say, "Fire one . . . fire two," the second torpedo hit around
midship, forward of the quarterdeck, somewhere in the close
vicinity of my Marine compartment. Then, a few seconds later, a
third explosion rocked the ship. It was the ammunition magazine
underneath me. The explosion blew all the way through the top
of number 1 turret—my bed the night before and, devastatingly,
Munson's bed that disastrous night. I'm sure he never felt a thing.
The detonations sent water high into the air, drenching me as
it rained down, yet protecting me from the massive fireball that
flared all around me. The blast was so powerful that the massive
turret with its three 18-foot barrels was lifted off its moorings
and sent over to the starboard side.

I was stunned and confused. No one was firing at us, and we
were not firing at anyone. I couldn't understand what was going
on. I looked toward the front of the ship and to my astonishment, it was gone! Approximately thirty-five feet of the bow
had disappeared. It had been completely cut off. I then realized
what had happened. We had been torpedoed.

Beneath me, below deck, I could hear and feel the bulkheads
breaking under the pressure of the water as the *Indy*'s gigantic
screw propellers continued to push her forward. Massive fires
from the explosions lit up the night sky, exposing the doomed
Indianapolis to any enemy that might still be lurking nearby.
All electrical power had been cut off. All communications had
been rendered inoperative. As a result, no word was sent to the

engine room to stop the engines. Within a minute of the initial blast, I had come to my senses and knew the ship was going to sink. The open bow was already going underwater.

I made my way to the emergency station, which was mid-ship on the quarterdeck. As I did, men were coming up from below deck, screaming cries of excruciating pain. Most were in their night skivvies and had been blown out of their bunks. Hysterically they cried for help. Many had scorched flesh hanging from their faces and arms. The smell of burning flesh and hair was nauseating. Compound fractures revealed protruding bones from the bodies of those who had been thrown up against the bulkhead walls. It was a living hell. I'll never forget the fires, the horrified faces, and the cacophony of screams. I can still hear the explosions and the screeching metal being twisted and torn by the tons of water the ship was taking on.

On my way to the emergency station, I noticed the ship was already listing about twenty degrees to the starboard. Evidently the second explosion had made a gaping hole in the starboard side, flooding most of the compartments in the forward area. As bulkheads continued to break, more and more water filled the lower compartments, causing the ship to actually erect itself for a minute or so. But as she continued to plow forward and bulkheads gave way, the ship rolled severely to starboard again. Because of CINCPAC's unwillingness to warn us of the high probability of imminent danger, we had been traveling completely open. Battle-ready status had been discouraged. Watertight doors were not closed and dogged. As unthinkable as it may be, the gallant *Indianapolis* and her noble crew had become victims not only of the enemy, but of the very Navy they served.

As best I can recall, it took me about four minutes to get to the emergency station. Realizing my kapok-filled life jacket was in the fiery inferno below deck in my locker, I was eager to get to the station where I knew many more were located. When I got there, I could see the canvas bags filled with jackets hanging all around on the open bulkheads. I yelled over to Lieutenant Stauffer, "Sir, permission to cut down the life jackets!" Committed to following Navy procedures, he quickly retorted, "No! Not until we are given orders to abandon ship!"

Suddenly, a Navy commander I recognized came from below deck—Commander Lipski. He was burned severely and pleading for help. At the sight of this, someone cried out, "Get the commander a life jacket!" Immediately a sailor cut down the canvas bags filled with kapoks. As they tumbled to the deck, I quickly grabbed one and put it on. I decided not to fasten it in the straddle, contemplating the jump I would soon have to make into the sea. Other sailors likewise scrambled for a jacket, each man knowing he was about to face the challenge of the great deep and perhaps soon meet his Creator and Judge. A controlled panic could be seen on every face as we suddenly found ourselves confronted with the very thing every human being hates—utter helplessness. Even so, the will to survive fortified itself with the face of bravery as we all desperately prepared to leap into the pitch-black water.

Another two or three minutes passed before word of mouth spread that Captain McVay had given the word to abandon ship. He had been waiting for a damage control report, but tragically, those who had gone below to make that assessment never made it back topside.

By now, men were being washed overboard. The front half of the ship was completely underwater. It was nearly impossible to stand on the open deck because of her severe list to starboard. When word to abandon ship finally reached the quarterdeck, many men ran to the high side (port side) and began jumping off. It was bedlam. In the light of the flames I could see men jumping on top of each other. I recall making my way to the port side and hanging on to the rail to keep from falling due to the steep incline. As I stood there, I looked out into the blackness of night and then at the pitch-black oil that had already started to leak from the *Indy* floating on the water below. That moment is indelibly etched in my mind. The stark reality of what was really happening flooded my senses. I was face-to-face with my mortality. Eternity was before me. And in the midst of my fear and helplessness, I cried out to God in prayer.

Anyone who has ever experienced a similar situation will understand what I am about to say: There are times when you pray, and times when you *pray*! This was one of those latter times. No one offered to help me because no one else *could* help me. I was there alone—or so it seemed. But as I reached out in desperation to the Savior of my soul, He suddenly made it clear to me that He was also going to be the Savior of my life. There was no audible voice. Something far more comforting was suddenly given to me. An unexplainable and ineffable peace enveloped me like a blanket on a frosty night. With the undeniable marks of the supernatural, the chill of terror was replaced with the glowing warmth of divine assurance. I knew within my heart that God was answering my prayers and was going to see me through.

As the finite security of the great *Indianapolis* slipped away beneath my feet, the infinite security of the Almighty bore me up and gave me peace—a supernatural peace promised in His Word: "Be anxious for nothing, but in everything by prayer and supplication with thanksgiving let your requests be made known to God. And the peace of God, which surpasses all comprehension, will guard your hearts and your minds in Christ Jesus" (Philippians 4:6–7).

Abandon Ship

With almost no one left on the quarterdeck, I stepped over the rail and walked two long steps down the side of the ship that now made a ramp into the water. Then I jumped feetfirst into the murky, oil-laden ocean. My kapok jacket came up over my head, and as I came up to the surface of the water, I desperately parted it with my hands in an effort to get my head above the layer of thick black oil. Pushing the oil away from my face, I swam away from the sinking ship about fifty yards and joined a few others who had also abandoned ship.

Together we watched in amazement as we saw the fantail going high in the air. As the ship went under, some boys who were still on board frantically ran up the fantail as it went vertical, but then it suddenly rolled to the starboard. In their panic, several boys blindly jumped off, landing in the four big screws that were still turning, and quickly met their death. Gradually the firelight of the steel inferno dimmed as the fantail disappeared. In a span of twelve minutes, the mighty USS *Indianapolis* slipped into her watery grave in the seven-mile depths of the Mariana Trench, the deepest region of the Pacific Ocean. There she rests to this day.

I cannot remember all that raced through my mind as I swam in the darkness, but I do recall a powerful promise that resonated within my heart that dreadful hour, a promise that has ruled my life from that day forward: "Peace I leave with you," Jesus said. "My peace I give unto you: not as the world giveth,

> I woke up when the torpedo hit. . . . Men were screaming all around and many were wounded. The ship listed to one side and I went into the ocean. After landing in the water, one of the planes started to roll over on me and another sailor. We finally got away from it. When we looked up we could see the *Indy* in the distance, plowing through the water on its side. The sky was all lit up with fire as it finally rolled over. I saw men on top, and the screws were still turning as it went straight down.
>
> Survivor John T. Heller

give I unto you. Let not your heart be troubled, neither let it be afraid" (John 14:27 KJV).

Survival is a powerful motivator. I looked around at some of my young shipmates. We took inventory of our little group and discovered there were about eighty of us. Since the *Indy* had continued to move ahead even after having been hit, many men had bailed off behind us, and some even in front of us. Small groups of men were scattered over approximately one mile. At least one-third of the men in my group were injured, some burned beyond recognition. Some men had no life jacket and hung on to their comrades who did. And to our dismay, there was not a life raft to be found. Our lives depended solely on divine providence and the kapok life vests He had supplied.

Two of my fellow Marines were in our little cluster of about eighty, but one had sustained such a serious injury after being blown against a bulkhead that he lasted only a couple of hours. The other Marine, Miles Spooner, dove into the water head-first when he abandoned ship, so his face was covered with the gooey oil. Over the next several days the oil would become an excruciating irritant to his eyes. As he tried to rub the oil out, he rubbed saltwater in. By the second day his eyes were so inflamed that he could not shut them. His eyeballs eventually bulged out of their sockets, leaving them vulnerable to the blistering sun and saltwater. Early on I knew he would never survive without help, so I gave him my word that I would be there for him, come what may.

By morning our numbers dwindled by about one-third. Most of the severely wounded were hysterical with high fevers and died during the night. When they passed on, we ceremonially removed their dog tags, a well-meaning but misguided act. We later learned that those who were given the macabre task of recovering the decomposed bodies had no way of knowing who they were. Seldom could they even acquire readable fingerprints—a determination only made possible by dehydrating the skin.

We also took their life jackets and gave them to crew members who were without. Then we quietly released their bodies into a watery grave. Even then, the corpses remained with us as if they were somehow still alive and afraid to leave. The gruesome sight of departed friends was a constant reminder of our potential fate and the fragility of life.

> My last view of the *Indianapolis* was bow down, flag still flying on the stern, and men jumping into the turning screws. Their screams still haunt me.
>
> Survivor John (Jack) C. Slankard

The First Day at Sea

The morning of July 30 brought with it both hope and despair. We were shivering cold and glad to feel the warmth of the rising sun. The surface water dropped to about eighty-five degrees Fahrenheit at night, gradually lowering our body temperatures to dangerous levels of hypothermia.

In *In Harm's Way*, Doug Stanton graphically describes the physiological processes of hypothermia, explaining that despite the comparative warmth of the Pacific Ocean at this latitude, it was still more than ten degrees cooler than the human body, which caused our core body temperatures to drop, often to dangerous levels.

Depending on the survivor's percentage of body fat and the clothes he was wearing (more clothes is better when it comes to retaining heat, even in water), each survivor was cooling at a slightly different rate. On average, as the air temperature dropped at night to the mid-eighties—which felt brutally cold compared to the hundred-degree days—our core body temperatures slipped about one degree for each hour we were in the water, and as much as ten degrees from sundown to sunup.

After sunset our bodies would begin shivering, which is normally the body's way of generating heat. Unfortunately, it also means you're burning four times more oxygen than normal. The body slows down to conserve energy. When the body cools to about ninety-three degrees, the central nervous system becomes depressed, apathy develops, speech becomes difficult, and amnesia occurs. At ninety-one degrees, urination stops as the kidneys stop filtering waste, and the body becomes poisoned. Finally, breathing becomes difficult, the heartbeat weakens, and you drift out of awareness of your surroundings.

71

Although he was not in our group, Dr. Lewis Haynes, one of the ship's doctors, later estimated that by Tuesday morning our temperatures were down to around eighty-five degrees. As the sun rose the next day, our body temperatures slowly rose with it, but little by little every night many survivors' temperatures sank lower and the day's sun wasn't able to catch them up. Eventually, they began hallucinating and lost the ability to make wise decisions, or their bodies shut down altogether.[13]

In an effort to keep us all together through the massive crests of waves, our dwindling little group formed a circle and fastened our life jackets to one another. Those who didn't have a jacket hung on to someone who did. If we had stayed on our own, we would have easily been separated by fifty yards in a matter of seconds.

For those of us who were able to talk, we naturally discussed the possibility of rescue. While no one knew for sure, we tried to assure ourselves that an SOS got off the ship. Even if it hadn't, surely the Navy would become alarmed when they discovered we failed to make our intended rendezvous the next day with the USS *Idaho*. Our hopes ebbed and flowed with the sound of every plane that flew over us, most at 30,000 feet.

The sunlight of the first day also brought with it a fear of being slaughtered by an enemy sub. Now vulnerable and easily seen, we knew that whoever torpedoed us could possibly still be around. We all surmised that we had been attacked by a Japanese sub, since we had never seen another ship. We also believed that their subs would surface and exterminate helpless men at sea with their machine guns (a cold-blooded order Hashimoto later said he would have never given). While another enemy attack was still a very real potential, I think most all of us had a guarded optimism that help was on its way. We told ourselves that the enemy would probably think the same thing, and therefore not want to linger in the area.

As the day dragged on, we continued to lose more boys. Those who had accidentally swallowed some of the oil had been vomiting all night and were now severely dehydrated and convulsing. They gradually became delusional and would thrash the waters and shake violently until they finally lost control of themselves. Most of these never made it through the first day.

As our bodies baked in the open sea, we began to realize that the sun was transitioning from friend to foe. It soon blistered our previously chilled and now exposed flesh. We tore our clothing to make protective hoods, but the ultraviolet rays reflecting off the water still managed to find our skin. The bright glare forced us to squint our eyes until our facial muscles became utterly exhausted. Our eyes also burned from the caustic saltwater waves that constantly splashed our faces.

Late on that first day, around dusk, we had company. To our horror, we saw several large black dorsal fins cutting through the water and circling our group. I cannot describe the fear of the anticipation and the unknown. But for some reason the sharks seemed unwilling to launch a full attack on our little cluster. They just circled around and around with what seemed to be a predetermination.

According to experts, the oceanic whitetip shark was most likely responsible for most of the attacks on our men. Growing up to ten feet long, they aren't the largest of sharks, but they are certainly large enough to become man-eaters when given the chance. They spend most of their time in the upper layer of the ocean but are one of the few species that prefers off-shore, deep-ocean areas. They are aggressive and competitive, and meals are likely to become feeding frenzies as many sharks go

> There were approximately two hundred or more [people in my] group. Sharks swam below us, bumping our legs. I am often asked about sharks. My reply: "They don't like Irishmen!" Most of us were Christians or became Christians. We prayed daily. God was with me always.
>
> Survivor Paul J. Murphy

after the same source of food. Another possible culprit could have been the tiger shark, which is darker and grows larger but is generally more likely to be solitary.

Sadly, some of the hallucinating boys insisted on swimming away from the group to an island or ship they were sure they saw. As they swam away, their thrashing often attracted the sharks and we'd hear a bloodcurdling scream. Like a fishing bobber taken under the water, the helpless sailor quickly disappeared. Then his mangled body would resurface moments later with only a portion of his torso remaining.

On other occasions the waves would tear one of the boys away from the group, causing him to helplessly drift into the shark-infested perimeter. Some of those men were only mauled and were able to make their way back to the group. Others were not so fortunate. Over the course of the next few days, this scenario would be played out more times than I wish to recount.

The Approaching Night

Certainly our resolve to do whatever we could to stay together was strengthened the first night. But our hopes of rescue seemed to sink with the setting of the sun. Incredible thirst and inexpressible fear of the sharks only worsened as the dark approached, dehydrated sailors continued to become incoherent and thrashed about until all their energy was depleted, and the thought of having to endure another shivering night was depressing. We were all miserable and helpless.

Desperation and fear only worsened as the blackness of night enveloped our quivering bodies. The darkness seemed to isolate us in our misery, preventing us from even seeing the guy next to us. For some of the men, there was nothing to bring hope. And without hope, all that is left is despair. But for me, hope never waned. And I do not say that to my credit, but to God's.

Growing up I was absolutely convinced God existed, but before reporting to boot camp, the reality of war and likelihood of my death began to grip my soul. I asked myself questions like, *Why was I placed here upon this earth? What is the real meaning of life? What if I don't make it back? Am I ready to stand before God and give an account of my life?*

Despite my church-going ways and other religious practices highly acceptable and expected in my Bible Belt culture, I realized I had no real relationship with God. He was distant, not personal. As a nineteen-year-old, I really had no faith, no passion to glorify God, no real hunger to hear the sound of His voice in Scripture and obediently serve Him, no real desire to commune with Him in prayer. I realized my best efforts fell far short of His standards. I was scared. My fear of death in war suddenly paled in insignificance. My sin condemned me to an eternal hell, and I knew it. I needed mercy. I needed forgiveness. I needed a Savior.

Racked with guilt and shame, the Lord, by His grace, drew me to himself in faith on the first day of August 1943 while I attended our little church in Murray, Kentucky. That Sunday after the sermon, the pastor gave an invitation and pronounced the benediction. Being deeply convicted that I had violated the laws of God in many ways, I remained seated as most everyone left. The pastor saw me and sat down by me and asked if he could help. I told him I needed to get things right with the Lord and that I felt as if today was my last chance. He opened his Bible and turned to Acts 16:31, which says, "Believe in the Lord Jesus, and you will be saved." In the quietness of that moment, by the regenerating power of the Holy Spirit, I begged God for His gift of mercy and grace, based solely on Jesus Christ paying for my sins on the cross. That day God forgave my sins, and I experienced the miracle of the new birth in Christ. Knowing the sinless Savior had taken my sins in exchange for His righteousness, my heart was filled with joy and relief. I remember thinking to myself, *Now I am ready for war, because now I am ready for eternity.*

Two years later, bobbing in the middle of the Pacific, I was reassured that even if the Lord chose to let me perish, I knew His sweet providence was ultimately in charge. In fact, it was a welcome thought to consider that He might decide to take me to my heavenly home and relieve me from my distress. But somehow I knew that He had plans for me and wanted me to survive.

Had it not been for the strength and incomprehensible peace of the Lord, I fear the ordeal of the first night and day would have destroyed me. I had already seen and experienced enough anguish and suffering to last me a lifetime. The inescapable bloody carnage alone was almost unbearable, not to mention my own physical challenges, plus the fear of the unknown. Yet through it all, God remained my close companion. His faithful presence gave me great strength and resolve.

As the terrors of the night surrounded me, my heart ran frequently to the Lord in prayer. The Holy Spirit would help me think of Scripture. When this happened, I would lay hold of His promises and pray them back to Him with an attitude of awe and great joy. That night I remember quoting the Twenty-third Psalm, giving special emphasis to the source of my strength and hope—the Lord himself—and to my Shepherd's personal care for me. I prayed:

> The LORD is *my* shepherd; *I* shall not want. *He* maketh *me* to lie down in green pastures: *he* leadeth *me* beside the still waters. *He* restoreth *my* soul: *he* leadeth *me* in the paths of righteousness for *his* name's sake. Yea, though *I* walk through the valley of the shadow of death, *I* will fear no evil: for *thou* art with *me; thy* rod and *thy* staff they comfort *me. Thou* preparest a table before *me* in the presence of mine enemies: *thou* anointest *my* head with oil; *my* cup runneth over. Surely goodness and mercy shall follow *me* all the days of *my* life: and *I* will dwell in the house of the LORD *for ever.*
>
> Psalm 23 KJV, emphasis mine

Sleep was intermittent during the night. Had it not been for sheer exhaustion, I probably never would have been able to even shut my eyes, much less doze off for short intervals. Yet by God's grace I relaxed in the darkness and rested in His care. Convinced that rescue would come in the morning, I felt encouraged and confident. Little did I know this was only the beginning. The worst was yet to come.

Then Jesus again spoke to them, saying, "I am the Light of the world; he who follows Me will not walk in the darkness, but will have the Light of life."

John 8:12

FOUR

Mysteries of Darkness and Light—the Second Day

Even before the sun peeked over the horizon that second day, I started to see the floating carnage of mutilated bodies around me. To my horror, numerous sailors with whom I had spoken the evening before were now facedown in the water.

At first I remained silent and still, paralyzed with disbelief. The eerie scene before me was like a floating battlefield on a calm sea. I tried hard to convince myself that some of my shipmates were just asleep. My eyes searched the emerging light to find life. Spooner and I had locked our legs around each other to preserve body heat through the night and avoid attracting sharks with dangling legs. But surely Spooner and I weren't the only ones left.

It became apparent that during the night our entire group had drifted apart considerably. The force of fifteen-foot swells had caused our life jacket fasteners to tear and fail. We also had to occasionally provide an exit for those in the inner circle

81

who died and those who became violent and wanted out due to saltwater hallucinations.

During those first minutes that early morning, I experienced feelings of loneliness I hope to never feel again in this life. But as the dawn continued to illumine the sea, we could see and hear others beginning to stir—a welcome relief. Gradually the silence was broken with much conversation and chatter. Some, however, began thrashing about in mental and physical agony. Others voiced the same concerns I had regarding men who appeared to be asleep. Slowly we swam toward our lifeless comrades to see if we could rouse them. Many had apparently succumbed to the chilling sleep of hypothermia.

While hypothermia claimed numerous victims, others who had sustained injuries aboard ship had also slipped into eternity after their long and constant battle swimming in the ocean, fighting the sharks and dehydration. Some of the dead had lost limbs from the torpedo explosion or were disemboweled by the sharks. I'm sure they welcomed death as a merciful reprieve from their excruciating pain. There were other boys, however, who were still alive but delusional, unable to speak coherently

Demented men were victims of shark fear—everyone became the enemy. One shouted, "There's Japanese on this line," and all hell broke loose. Men were stabbing the people next to them, fighting with whoever was close. Toward morning it became quiet. I guess those of us who remained became exhausted to a point of no return.

Survivor Frank J. Centazzo

or act rationally. Most were now too weak to scream. From them, only the sounds of faint groans or calls to God for mercy could be heard.

The scenes of that morning are forever etched in my mind. The inexpressible feelings of despair brought many of us to the very edge of suicide. I'm sure some of those who had passed through the veil of this life had chosen that option. Too exhausted to hold their heads up and out of the water, they simply gave up.

My buddy Spooner wanted to take his life. By now, after having rubbed and rubbed his eyes with oil and saltwater, he was unable to close his eyes. They had become two ulcerated sores, and the slightest ray of light triggered enormous pain. Obviously, the sunrise was virtually unbearable, making suicide a viable alternative. "Harrell," he said to me. "We know no help is coming, and I can't stand this pain much longer." He repeated this several times throughout the day. I recall asking him how he would end his life, to which he replied, "I'll dive down so far that I'll drown before I come back up."

I knew he was miserable, but I simply could not stand the thought of letting him go. So I continuously had to talk him out of it. Tapping deep into my own hope of survival and my pride of being a United States Marine, I told him, "Spooner, listen to me. There are only two Marines left in this group, and when everyone else is gone, I'm still going to be here and you're going to be with me. I know in my heart that God is going to deliver us and we are going to survive this together." He gave no reply, but somehow I sensed that my confidence got to him. Unsure of what he was thinking, I turned his back to me and assertively fastened his kapok jacket to mine. He seemed to relax at that point, probably more out of exhaustion than relief.

I tried to convince myself that today we would be rescued. Surely the Navy was combing the ocean surface to find us by now, and rescue planes would be hovering over us at any moment. To think otherwise would only fan the embers of desperation into a raging fire of hopelessness.

As I felt my body becoming increasingly frail, my mind returned to that moment two nights earlier when I hung on to the ship's rail just before I abandoned ship. I reflected upon the supernatural peace that God gave me through His unfailing promise—*I will never leave you nor forsake you.* Inevitably that assurance would give me strength. God's Holy Spirit within me would bring to mind Bible verses that I would repeat over and over throughout those days and nights. In fact, as I think back on how His written Word provided comfort and hope, I more fully appreciate the words of the psalmist: "Your word is a lamp to my feet and a light to my path" (Psalm 119:105).

Thirst and Hallucination

Our group had dwindled from eighty the first day to about forty by noon the second day. It was a constant battle to round up stragglers and care for the wounded.

As a result of the rising sun combined with the increased activity of releasing the dead from their kapok jackets, we warmed up quickly. But the warmth made us even more desperate for water. By the time the sun reached its zenith at midday, our lips were cracked and bleeding and our tongues were beginning to swell in our parched mouths and throats, making our speech slurred almost beyond understanding. Dehydration was becoming our new and dreaded enemy—one that had taken the place of the sharks that would come and go. The

I am not overly religious, but I called on my Maker as earnestly as any young fellow ever did. I am sure all the others did the same. Lying there in the middle of the Pacific Ocean with nothing but water in sight reminded me of the line, "Water, water, everywhere, but not a drop to drink."

Survivor James B. Loftis

only answer for the dehydration was the one thing we did not have—fresh water. We were floating in a close substitute, but it was one that would kill. There are no words to describe such a strange torture, and it proved to be too strong a temptation for some to withstand.

A rash of mass hallucination began to plague our group with devastating results. With our minds becoming unhinged, our tongues swollen, and our throats squeezing shut, it's easy to understand why some of the survivors began drinking the saltwater. They'd resisted for so long that what began as furtive sipping soon turned into joyous gulps, as their bleeding lips sucked up the cool water around them.

Dr. Haynes later described for author Doug Stanton what he saw from a medical perspective:

As they drank, the boys were setting off a complex series of chemical reactions, all of them volatile. The sea contains twice the salinity that the human body can safely ingest, and as the boys drank, their cells were shrinking, expanding, and exploding as they sacrificed what's called their "free water." This was the cells' attempt to lower the sodium deluging the bloodstream, and it was futile. [1]

At that point their kidneys would try desperately to clean the blood before sending it back into circulation, but the sodium would be too much for them. When a body is overcome by an excess of salt, it succumbs to what is known as hypernatremia. A root-beer-colored liquid foams out of the nose, and the victim's eyes roll back in his head. Breathing becomes more difficult, lips turn blue, and the brain's neurons misfire or stop firing altogether. At this point the brain is like a car battery that's not working properly, as its power cells have been altered. Then, as the brain misfires, it leads to more bad decision-making, becoming an endless, destructive loop. The only cure is to rehydrate the victim quickly and thoroughly.

The boys who fell into this trap soon had violent fits, whooping and hollering and twisting around in the water with flailing arms. Suddenly, as if an explosion had taken place, they would fall into a coma and go limp. Sometimes this would happen in the middle of a ring of sharks.

Some would lay there, floating motionlessly, while others jerked around in terror, clawing the air in silent panic, their throats too dry to scream. They would only live a few hours.

Dealing with hallucinating friends was extremely difficult. It was like trying to reason with an angry drunk or a disoriented Alzheimer's patient—the saltwater making them crazy. Occasionally a hallucinating shipmate would attack another sailor close to him. The delusional sailor would convince himself that his buddy was the enemy and go after him with a vengeance. Others would assault a shipmate, thinking he was hiding fresh water.

On several occasions hallucinating sailors claimed to see a ship or an island and excitedly tried to enlist others to swim with them to safety. We tried to form a human circle to corral those who were the most demented, but eventually the most desperate men would break through, chasing after a mirage of an oasis that didn't exist. By the second day, fatigue had set in, making it difficult to expend extra energy on the delirious sailors. In our weakened condition, we were unable to fight the swells, so little by little our circle of safety deteriorated into a scattered flotilla of helpless men adrift. It was basically every man for himself. Nevertheless, we tried to reason with our irrational mates, even if it was, at times, an exercise in futility.

Inevitably, when we disagreed with them or attempted to calm them, they would become belligerent and often vicious. Invectives would spew forth from confused and angry hearts. I would try to apply Scripture when I spoke to them, remembering that "a gentle answer turns away wrath, but a harsh word stirs up anger" (Proverbs 15:1). Kindness and agreement would occasionally calm them down, but only temporarily. It was exhausting to try and prevent them from hysterically swimming away from the group. Those who left the safety of the group would soon begin to flail about in the waters, struggling with fatigue and insanity. This, of course, would draw the attention of the sharks. Soon we would hear a bloodcurdling scream of terror and watch the helpless victim disappear, then surface again with his remains being fought over by other sharks—a haunting sound and scene I cannot erase from my mind.

I vividly remember an incident on that day with a sixteen-year-old sailor who had been aboard ship less than three weeks. He lied about his age in order to join the Navy (along with his twin brother who was also on board but not in our group). Dehydration had taken its toll on him. Like others before him, he began to get increasingly excited, flailing and splashing about, looking around with a nervous enthusiasm. Seeing me, he swam over and insisted, "The scuttlebutt is open!"—Navy talk for access to a drinking fountain aboard ship. Frantically he stuck his face into the water and pointed down at his fantasy. No reasoning to the contrary would dissuade him. He was utterly convinced of his salvation. Screaming hysterically with jubilation, he removed his life vest and all his clothes. Because he had not been aboard ship long enough to get a suntan, his body was lily-white. I can still see him slowly disappear into the depths of the Pacific as he swam after a figment of his imagination.

As the day wore on, hope continued to wane for all of us. A man can endure just about anything as long as he has hope. But take away his hope, and all that is left is despair and the relief of suicide. We frequently saw planes flying overhead, but they were flying at 30,000 feet. Many of them were our B-29 bombers on bombing missions to Japan. Gradually we figured we just had to tune them out and ignore them.

Prayer Meeting at Sea

Although my understanding of spiritual issues was immature and my faith largely untested as a young man, I still possessed an unwavering assurance that I would be saved, both physically and spiritually. I did not fully understand it at the time, but my confidence emanated from the Holy Spirit within me.

Only God knows how many other men shared my faith and experienced the same spiritual assurance. Certainly many, if not most, of the men prayed. Their prayers would sound something like this: "God, if you're out there somewhere, we need your help. I don't want to die. None of us want to die. I have a family back home. Please save us!" Seldom would they close with an "amen" because the unbearable pathos of their hearts would overflow into uncontrollable sobbing. The vividness of these memories is still a source of perpetual grief for me.

As the day wore on, I continued to pray and quote portions of Scripture that came to mind. Verses such as "The steadfast of mind You will keep in perfect peace, because he trusts in You" (Isaiah 26:3) brought comfort to my aching heart.

Answered Prayer in a Cloud

The monotony of the waves was mesmerizing. Over and over again, the lumbering swells hoisted us high into the air and then gently lowered us into the infinite valleys of the Pacific. But we continued to pray.

After many hours of persistent supplication, a possible answer seemed to appear in the distance. It was a small, dark cloud—a harbinger of life-giving water. I can still visualize that little cloud drawing closer and closer. Eventually we could see rain falling from it. Our hearts pounded within us as we begged God to steer it over to our gaping mouths. With swollen tongues we cried out to God for just a few drops of the life-sustaining fluid. Within a matter of minutes, our prayers

I prayed silently for the first time in my life. Don't let anyone tell you he cannot pray; even an atheist cannot deny the existence of God. We prayed to God to ease our pains. We prayed to God not to forsake us, not to let us die, to save us. The soothing effects of prayer linked us together as we began to try to help each other.

Survivor Buck W. Gibson

were answered. The fresh, cool water beat hard against our sunburned faces. We used our hands to funnel as much water as we could into our parched mouths. I remember weeping with joy as I opened my mouth heavenward and drank freely from His kind provision.

But when the brief rain shower was over, the sun once again glared down on our sunburned bodies. Our eyelids were severely swollen and the moisture on our lips quickly dissipated in the hot sun, leaving them exposed, cracked, and bleeding. The membranes of our eyes and noses were also highly irritated. Most of the boys were nearly blind.

I cut the sleeves out of my dungaree jacket and spread them over my face, not only for protection from the sun, but also to prevent the dangerous saltwater from splashing into my nose and mouth and strangling me. I knew I had to avoid drinking it at all cost, so I constantly fought the turbulent waves to avoid being strangled. Occasionally the poisonous saline would catch me a bit off guard and I would end up with a mouthful. I would immediately begin to gag for my very life—a task that required me to expend precious energy.

Desperate for water, some boys would tear off a piece of clothing, hold it over his mouth, and have a buddy scoop water into the cloth, foolishly thinking they were straining out at least some of the salt. Soon they too would become prey for the sharks that were always lingering close by. Those who were married with families fought harder to avoid the temptation to drink. Many later admitted that visions of their wives and family kept them alive. But many others had nothing to restrain them from risking their lives with such a silly experiment.

The scene around me on that second day can only be likened to a nightmare. Human remains and corpses continued to float all around our dwindling group. The sharks were never far away, lingering in the distance, occasionally picking off a straggler.

Those of us who could still see remember with horror those black dorsal fins slicing through the water. When they would swim through our ranks, hysteria would naturally overwhelm us. It was probably even worse for those nearly blind who could hear the terrifying screams but were unable to clearly see the ferocious predator. On numerous occasions I recall seeing a large fin coming straight at me. In horror I would take what I thought would be my last breath, bend my knees up to my chest, and cry out, "O God, help!" Sometimes I could feel a fin brush my body. Other times I would merely feel the wake of the massive beast streaking through the water just underneath me. These gut-wrenching encounters caused me to feel as though I was constantly tied up in a knot.

Excruciating body cramps would often follow these episodes. Every muscle fiber in my body would tense up to make me as small a target as I could possibly become. When the sharks were active, my weakened body would finally get to a point where I could no longer draw my knees up to my chest. My abdominal muscles would become completely exhausted,

A shark got one of my buddies who was just a couple feet from me. The shark's tail and the water just covered me up—I was that close. If the sharks took a man's leg, or just bit him, sometimes he would float back up; some did and some didn't. Of course, they were all dead. We'd take their life jackets and their dog tags.

Survivor Loel Dene Cox

leaving my legs to helplessly dangle in the path of the mighty marauders.

By God's providence I was spared from the sharks, but the trauma of those encounters later manifested itself in what was diagnosed as the most severe case of pelvic lipomatosis the doctors had ever seen. They believed that the prolonged exposure to cold water combined with the torturous stress of extreme panic had ultimately caused a lipoma (a benign tumor of fat tissues) to form in and around my colon, bladder, and stomach cavity, resulting in major surgery years later.

The winds and the sea began to pick up later that afternoon and evening. We were steadily losing a sailor every few hours. Our weakened bodies were no match for the powerful ocean. We would have given anything for even a raft. Unable to swim and stay together, our shrinking group was systematically dispersed over several hundred yards as night began to fall.

By now our kapok jackets were losing their buoyancy. They were not designed to keep a man afloat for more than forty-eight hours. As they became water-logged, our bodies naturally rode deeper in the water, putting us at even greater risk of strangulation and drowning. Little did we know that eventually we would have to remove them altogether and try to sit on them in order to keep our heads out of the water—a balancing act that would require even more of our waning energy. Making it worse, the rough canvas on what was commonly referred to as "the horse collar" had become an irritant to our necks, chins, and other body parts where it was free to rub. These rubs became raw and infected sores due to the saltwater and oil. Saltwater ulcers, as they were called, were also being added to the list of tortures. Open wounds began to develop in every fold of skin on our bodies. Those at the bend of the arm, the armpit, and behind the knees were the worst for me.

I met a friend who had a rubber belt like mine. We stuck together, telling each other we would make it and not to give up. We took turns sleeping while the other made sure he stayed awake. After three or four days, he looked at me and said, "I can't take this anymore." We started to pray, and that is when he gave me his life belt. He went down. I tried, but I could not reach him.

Survivor Lindsey L. Carter

Some of the boys were wearing air-filled rubber life belts instead of kapok jackets. But they soon discovered that most of them leaked. Before the *Indy* had sunk, many had worn the rubber belts, uninflated, during combat as a precaution in case they had to suddenly abandon ship. If that happened, they could inflate the belt and hopefully remain afloat until they were rescued. Unfortunately, the prolonged exposure to sunlight aboard ship caused the rubber to dry-rot and crack, greatly reducing their ability to retain air for any sustained period. Worse yet, a rubber belt around the waist has a tendency to throw the body into a prone position rather than holding it erect. The poor boys who wore them were always fighting to stay upright.

As darkness deepened and the seas churned, hope of rescue continued to wane. By the end of the second day, our group had dwindled to around thirty. And now we faced another shivering night, lost at sea.

W ho gives the sun for light by day
     And the fixed order of the moon
   and the stars for light by night,
Who stirs up the sea so that its waves roar;
The LORD of hosts is His name.

Jeremiah 31:35

 CHAPTER
FIVE

From Light to Starless Night— the Third Day

Hypothermia increased its grip as the hours passed during the third night. As if floating in an immense dungeon filled with cool water, I found myself fighting to remain sane. The chilling numbness of body and soul would cause me to drift in and out of reality. At times it was hard to know if I was dreaming or if I was indeed hopelessly adrift in the deepest part of the Pacific Ocean. But the sounds of the night had a way of quickly jarring me back to reality.

Off and on, all through the night, I could hear dying sailors thrashing around in the water as their bodies succumbed to the insanity of saltwater poisoning. The crazy, incoherent jabber describing some hallucination in their mind was always a certain indication that they would soon be gone. Every hour there seemed to be at least one or two who were out of control, swimming around with no idea where they were going. It was futile to try and help them. They seemed to have superhuman strength in the final, frenzied minutes of their lives, making it dangerous to get near them for fear that they would pull us under with them. We all knew it was best to merely stay away from them and conserve what little energy we had left.

The sharks remained with us that night. Though we could not see them, we occasionally felt their wake, and at times, their actual bodies. This, of course, would trigger horrific screams of panic. It was bedlam—a nightmare of death and dying. Needless to say, it was almost impossible to sleep, though our bodies were beyond exhausted. Spooner and I continued to fasten our kapok jackets together and lock our legs around each other for stability and warmth, and also to keep our feet and legs from dangling in the water in an effort to attract as little attention from the sharks as possible. Occasionally, when things would die down for a few minutes, we could doze off briefly and relax—only to be reawakened after a short time by more screams and thrashing.

Eventually the darkness of night gave way to dawn. Once again, the sun was a welcome relief to our shivering bodies. It was hard to imagine that we were now beginning our third day at sea. My mind continued to vacillate between hope and despair. Sometimes I would think positively, assuring myself that a search and rescue operation was combing the ocean for us and would soon find us.

I would think of my family and friends back home, and smile as I thought about my girlfriend in Murray, Kentucky. I would convince myself that we would all soon be reunited. Then my hopes would give way to reality as my weakening condition and the floating carnage all around me gave irrefutable evidence that I could not hang on much longer. Yet in the midst of my inner anguish, God would always have the final say. In ways I cannot explain, He brought a supernatural peace and assurance to my desperate soul. God was ever so faithful to His promise found in Philippians 4:6–7: "Be anxious for nothing, but in everything by prayer and supplication with thanksgiving let your requests be made known to God. And the peace of God, which surpasses all comprehension, shall guard your hearts and your minds in Christ Jesus."

The morning light of the third day revealed that our numbers had now dwindled to only seventeen—a mere fraction of the original eighty or so in my group. As usual, the seas were rough, tossing us around like rubber balls. Back and forth we rocked in a torturous rhythm that only added to our fatigue. The decaying bodies of deceased shipmates floated along with us, but none of them were recognizable. The flesh on their faces had already decomposed. With cheekbones protruding and mere holes for eye sockets, they bore no resemblance to anything human. Their presence only added to the torture of our miserable existence because we knew that unless help came soon, we would become just like them. Yet despite the gruesome reality of having them drift along with us, in some strange way they were still welcomed. It's strange how war and suffering unites the spirits of men in an inseparable bond. I feel that powerful bond even today.

As the sun grew brighter and began to bear down upon us, our parched throats and tongues swelled so badly that we could hardly talk. There was really nothing to say anyway. But we all needed encouragement and hope just to keep our wits about us and pass the time. So we began to pray once again. From about 10:00 a.m. to 1:00 p.m. (the fact that I could see the passage of time was both a blessing and a curse; the watch I wore still works today, and is now on display in the Indiana War Memorial Museum in Indianapolis), each man poured his heart out to

> By this time I would have given up my front seat in heaven and walked the rotten log all the way through hell for just one cool drink of water. My mouth was so dry it was like cotton. How I got up enough nerve to take a mouthful of saltwater, rinse my mouth, and spit it out, I don't know, but I did—did it a couple of times before the morning was over. That's probably why I ended up with saltwater ulcers in my throat. When we got picked up, my throat was bigger than my head.
>
> Survivor Woodie E. James

his Maker, begging Him for physical deliverance and promising spiritual reformation in return. Mingled with our prayers were passionate conversations describing our families and friends back home. Some of the men were almost gone, unable to even get a sound past their throats. Others were in varying stages of hallucination due to saltwater poisoning. But those who could, prayed.

Gone was the attitude of pride that deceives men into thinking that there is no God, or if there is, they don't need Him. When a man is confronted with death, it is the face of Almighty God he sees, not his own. We were all acutely aware of our Creator during those days and nights. Our little seventeen-member prayer meeting attested to this. Every man knew he was dying. It was only a matter of hours. Only a miracle could save us. So we prayed for a miracle.

Men prayed like I have never heard men pray. With inconsolable grief each man who was able to talk poured out his heart to God. With swollen tongues we did our best taking turns pleading with God for deliverance. And before one could finish, another would interrupt with *his* supplications. Another would then speak of his wife and children, and then cry out to God to be reunited with them. Because of dehydration, there were very few tears rolling down our grimacing faces. It was as though the ocean now contained them all.

A Makeshift Raft

The prayer meeting was emotionally exhausting. As things got quiet among us, we once again surrendered to the sea in an almost catatonic stupor. Silently we floated, back and forth. Up and down. Curious sharks would periodically make their way through our ranks, slowly and deliberately, only to disappear without incident.

While I have no way of knowing the minds of my comrades, certainly for me there still remained a glimmer of hope hidden away in some secret recess of my heart. The indwelling Spirit of God, my resident Comforter, continued to give me the perfect measure of grace to bear up under the weight of despair. I frequently obeyed the admonition to "come boldly unto the throne of grace, that we may obtain mercy, and find grace to help in time of need" (Hebrews 4:16 KJV).

Within minutes after our prayer time concluded, we ascended a large swell, and to our amazement we could see in the distance what appeared to be a makeshift raft surrounded by a few men. Before then we had figured there must be others out there somewhere, but we had no way of knowing for sure. We could faintly hear some chatter and knew that it had to be some of ours. After making contact, both of our little groups gradually made our way toward a central rendezvous. As we got closer

to them, I could see that there was no one on the raft, but five
sailors were swimming and pulling the little raft ever so slowly
in our direction. We were elated to know that at least there were
a few others who had survived.

After exchanging some very warm greetings, we learned that
they were trying to swim to the Philippines, thinking that if they
could get a little closer to the islands they would be more likely
to be spotted. As they came alongside our group, we could see
that the raft was actually two 40 mm ammunition cans and
four wood-slatted potato or orange crates all lashed together
with strips of cloth. Tied to the top was a real answer to our
prayers—several kapok life jackets that had been removed from
deceased boys and placed atop the little flotilla to dry out. This
meant that we had spare jackets for when ours played out—an
immediate concern. Due to logistics and sheer lack of energy, no
one could possibly hoist themselves onto the raft, but I accepted
this situation of meeting other survivors as a gift from God.

The sailors with the raft were quite adamant that no one was
looking for us, otherwise we would already have been rescued.
Although none of us wanted to admit it, down deep we all
agreed. In light of this stark reality, they had decided to swim
toward the Philippines—five hundred miles to the west, though
we didn't know the distance or exact direction at the time. Their
logic was simple: The closer they got to the Philippines, the
greater their chance of being spotted and rescued.

They asked if any of us wanted to join them. Seeing the
kapok jackets drying in the sun on the raft, and not having
a better alternative, I immediately said to my Marine buddy
Spooner, "I'm going to join them." He responded, "If you go,
Harrell, I'm going with you." So we left our little group—two
Marines joining five sailors, heading for the Philippines. We

> On the third or fourth day, our life jackets became saturated. More men were lost. We had to turn their life lines loose, as they would have pulled us down. More and more men turned to prayer. Several sang the "Navy Hymn," which we had sung every Sunday morning aboard ship . . . "for those in peril on the sea."
>
> Survivor William R. Mulvey

said our farewells to the fifteen sailors we had been with, all of them convinced my new little group would never survive such a foolhardy venture. To my knowledge, that is the last I ever saw of them.

With a renewed sense of direction and welcome buoyancy from the drier kapok jackets, we grabbed hold of the strings and pieces of cloth that lashed our little flotilla together and set a course for the Philippines. Ever so gently we cupped our hands and stroked the water while our fatigued legs did their best to kick. I'm sure that most of our progress was only in our minds, but at least it gave us some sense of taking charge of our situation. Refusing to admit the magnitude of the task before us, we stroked and kicked, making headway for a time. However, our weakened bodies soon proved to be no match for the force of the ocean. Nevertheless, we forged ahead with a determined spirit, and were soon out of sight of our shipmates.

Divine Provision

As the sun was sinking in the west, about three or four hours after we had joined our Philippine-bound comrades, we noticed something on the water about two hundred yards forward and off to the right about one hundred yards. At first it looked as though it may have been one of our boys. But as favorable swells helped us get closer, we began to make out what appeared to be floating debris or perhaps a partially submerged crate bobbing on the surface. Having not seen any sharks for several hours, I insisted on swimming out to investigate. I really felt compelled to go, even though it meant spending reserved energy.

As I slowly made my way to the strange debris, I remember praying something like, *Lord, please let there be food in this crate. Please provide. You alone are our hope.* As I got closer, it became obvious that indeed it was a wooden crate. The top was partly open and I could see that there were potatoes floating inside. I thanked the Lord for His provision while frantically reaching for the sustenance. As I grabbed hold of the first potato, my heart nearly stopped beating as I realized it was rotten. But as I squeezed it in torment, I found that it was solid on the inside. The rot oozed through my fingers as I compressed the precious spud until my palm felt the hard inner core, which I quickly popped into my mouth. Then I grabbed another and used my teeth to hurriedly peel away the putrefying outer layer, and devoured it as well. To my delight the crate was half full of potatoes—rotten on the outside, but to a starving young man, delicious on the inside. Once again the Lord had come to our rescue. The day before He provided water; now He provided food.

With great rejoicing I praised the Lord for His provision. I felt a renewed confidence that He would answer my greater prayer of ultimate rescue. After eating only three or four of the half-rotten potatoes, I felt that I was full, so I began stuffing all the potatoes I could in the pockets of my dungarees. With the smile of a conquering general, I grabbed the crate and made my way back to my shipmates. As I got within earshot of them, they began hollering, "What is it? What took you so long?" I hollered back, "Potatoes—half-rotten potatoes!" I'll never forget the joy on their faces when we all gathered around that little wooden dinner table.

There had been few circumstances to be happy about since we had entered the water, but the Lord changed all that with those potatoes—at least for a short while. Although our physical condition would not allow us to eat much, we ate enough to give us at least a little nourishment and a whole lot of encouragement.

Nightfall—the Fourth Night

With renewed zeal fueled by a few morsels of food and perhaps a tablespoon of water, we entered into our fourth night. It was now Wednesday evening, some sixty-six hours since we first entered the water at midnight on Sunday. As the sun began to set, we noticed the skies were becoming overcast. While the darkness of night gave relief from the burning sun, it was always a foreboding prospect.

Darkness naturally casts a spell upon man, even in the best of times. But darkness at sea is especially ominous, even more so on an overcast night when the clouds obscure the hope-giving luminaries of the moon and stars. Without light, you are unable to see anything, including the horizon. The blackness of the night wraps itself around you with an infinite darkness, causing a surreal disorientation and profound isolation. This, combined with the menacing sharks, produced a level of fear that was numbing. It was as if we were corpses suspended somewhere between life and death. Naturally, without the moon and stars, we had no compass. And without a view of the Southern Cross constellation, we had no way to determine our bearing and continue our imaginary progress toward the Philippines. We had no choice but to merely hang on to the raft and let the great ocean take us where it would.

Since that dreary night, I never take for granted the glory and majesty of God displayed in the moon and stars He created. "Who gives the sun for light by day, and the fixed order of the moon and the stars for light by night, who stirs up the sea so that its waves roar; The LORD of hosts is His name" (Jeremiah 31:35).

Voices Piercing the Darkness

I don't recall much of what happened as the night wore on, not until around midnight when the sound of voices suddenly pierced the darkness. We knew it must be some of our ship-mates, so we began to yell out to them, triggering an immediate response.

Gradually they made their way over to our little flotilla. Because of the darkness, I'm not sure to this day how many there were. They came straggling in one or two at a time. I think there may have been five or six. We were all drifting around the raft for some time, talking and not really knowing what to do. They too were proposing to swim closer to the Philippines in hopes of being spotted.

There was one naval officer in the group that I immediately recognized. He was Lieutenant McKissick. I had stood watch on the bridge for the captain when Lieutenant McKissick was the officer of the deck. I had learned to really appreciate him aboard ship. He was from Texas, and he was a peach of a guy. He made it easier for me to relay messages to the captain and would often repeat them to me to make sure that I had them right before he sent me off.

After a few minutes of conversation, it was obvious that the lieutenant was in charge. He deserved that not only because of rank, but also because of his winsome character. Men automatically respected him. I couldn't hold back the fact that I still had a pocket full of half-rotten potatoes, so I shared them with our reunited shipmates. As you might well imagine, they gladly ate them, half-rotten though they were.

Together both groups discussed plans to press on toward the Philippines. At first, Lieutenant McKissick seemed a bit reluctant to proceed ahead encumbered by the raft. Yet the prospect of extra life jackets was also a fact worthy of serious consideration. So we agreed to push on, raft and all. What happened after that is lost forever in my memory. Somewhere in the early hours of that fourth morning while it was still black as pitch, I became separated from the raft and most of my shipmates, including my Marine buddy Spooner. The next thing I remember occurred on the morning of the fourth day.

My kapok jacket had become so water-logged that it would no longer keep my head above water. At some point I had taken it off, turned it upside down, and sat on it. I remember having to constantly paddle with my hands to hold myself erect, otherwise the jacket had just enough buoyancy to flip me over, which it did on numerous occasions. I also recall looking frantically for Spooner, but he was nowhere to be found. I was too weak to yell, and I believed it wouldn't do any good anyway. I was convinced he had perished, and I battled the possibility that I soon would do the same. Apart from the unfailing presence of my Lord, I had only two companions with me that morning—one sailor, whose head was already facedown in the water, and Lieutenant McKissick.

I became increasingly confused that morning. On the one hand, I remained convinced that somehow God would rescue me. But on the other hand I knew that I had been lost at sea for four days. My original group of eighty had now diminished to only one other man. All I could see around me was human carnage. I could literally taste the stench of rotting flesh floating here and there on the surface. Curious sharks continued to appear and disappear. From time to time I could see their fins slicing through the water and occasionally watch them pass beneath me. By this time, I was too exhausted to be afraid. It was during the early morning hours of the fourth day that reality caused me to reevaluate my perspective. My hope of surviving was waning and I began to entertain the possibility that the Lord was going to rescue me in a different way. I started thinking that perhaps He would deliver me not only from the sea, but from life on earth altogether. Yet somehow the will to survive would not let me give up.

What happened next can only be described as an amazing display of divine sovereignty—an unbelievable series of events that not only saved my physical life, but also set into motion the rescue of many souls who have, because of this testimony, also placed their trust in the Savior.

Since I am afflicted and needy,
Let the Lord be mindful of me.
You are my help and my deliverer;
Do not delay, O my God.

Psalm 40:17

 CHAPTER

SIX

Ducks on the Pond—
the Fourth Day

My memories are limited as I reflect upon the fourth morning. I was so weak that I could barely move my arms and hands to help me stay seated on my water-logged kapok jacket. I was besieged with thoughts of surrendering to the sea. Yet I am certain that the Lord's all-seeing eye remained fixed on me as my impoverished body bobbed atop the massive ocean. As Psalm 139:9–10 promises, "If I dwell in the remotest part of the sea, even there Your hand will lead me, and Your right hand will lay hold of me." Certainly the ministering spirits of His angelic host were actively engaged in my survival, for by now, I was almost gone. While I could not see them, I am sure they protected me.

Then my mind would suddenly transcend my desperate state and become fixated on thoughts of my mom and dad, my six brothers and two sisters, and my girlfriend waiting for me in the beautiful rolling hills of western Kentucky. Immediately such thoughts would invigorate me to push on. With renewed determination I would tell myself, *I can't give up now. Lord, help me not to give up!*

It was hard to look at the dead sailor drifting along with us—a man I never even knew. It was as though I was looking at myself in a few hours. I couldn't bear to think about him and the family that would mourn him. Instead, I forced myself to look only at the living. McKissick was now my only live companion. Unable to see or hear anyone else, I assumed we were the last to still be alive. Although I beat myself up at times for leaving the raft to follow him, I always end up convincing myself that I did the right thing. After all, I needed to follow someone. And I was certainly in no condition to lead. Besides, McKissick had promised to take me to the Philippines!

For reasons I cannot explain, I remember referring to him as "Uncle Edwin"—one of my dad's brothers and a close friend back in Kentucky. I suppose my borderline delirious condition, combined with wishful thinking, caused me to project upon McKissick the image of someone safe, strong, and part of the family I longed to see. Together, we struggled to stay together that fourth morning. This was a formidable task given the ten- to

> On the morning of the fourth day, there were even fewer of us. I counted forty people and four rafts. Then I decided that most of the forty were out of their minds. I rounded up ten who seemed to be sane enough, and we took one raft and separated from the rest. It was getting too difficult to sort out the hallucinations and the real world. . . . It was a raw case of survival of the fittest.
>
> Survivor Donald J. Blum

twelve-foot swells that gently lifted us high, only to lower us once again into the depths of the saline valleys. The hypnotic rhythm of the waves only added to my body's craving for sleep. On several occasions I dozed off momentarily, only to be awakened by the frightening reality of tumbling off my life-saving seat.

On one such occasion, later on that fourth morning, I was aroused from a thirty-second catnap by something far more terrifying. Suddenly, something hit me and splashed water all around me. I was knocked off my little perch and sent flailing into the water. My instant reaction was that another shark had bumped me. I tried frantically to get my life jacket back down under me before he could return. Desperately my exhausted muscles fought the water until I got back into the only secure position available to me—as laughable as that may seem.

When I finally got seated again, I looked, and to my astonishment a million little fish swarmed all around me. These little creatures, about twelve inches long, were everywhere. They were constantly nudging me as they darted back and forth. Evidently I was a curiosity to them, and they certainly were a welcome sight to me. They were a pleasant relief from the sharks I had anticipated! Furiously I tried to catch them with my hands, but to no avail. Whenever I moved, they would all move, as if they were one giant organism. Somehow that little encounter brought much-needed encouragement to me. I suppose it distracted me a bit, causing me to focus on life rather than death.

Sighted!

Only the marvelous providence of God can account for what happened next. Unknown to us, Lt. Chuck Gwinn was flying overhead in a Lockheed Ventura PV-1 bomber used to search and destroy Japanese submarines. As Gwinn patrolled the waters at about three thousand feet, a recurring problem with a weighted antenna sock, of all things, set our unexpected sighting in motion. The sock was used to prevent the long whip antenna from flailing about. For some reason the troublesome sock had come off, causing the antenna to whip back and forth against the side of the plane—a potentially dangerous situation. Gwinn decided to leave the cockpit and assist his bombardier, Joe Johnson, in coming up with a remedy for the problem. As he looked out the bomb bay window in the floor of the airplane to consider a creative solution, his ever vigilant and well-trained eyes unexpectedly fell upon some tiny shining objects on the water below. Looking more closely, he noticed what he thought was some kind of discoloration on the water. He hurriedly climbed back into the cockpit and dropped down for a closer look, thinking perhaps it was an oil slick from a wounded enemy submarine.

By the time he reached about three hundred feet, to their amazement, the crew began to detect the oil-soaked heads of men scattered in twos and threes, their heads bobbing on the water. In fact, the water was filled with debris, corpses, and empty kapok life jackets mingled among many sharks. Then they spotted about thirty greasy survivors splashing and waving—fellow survivors that McKissick and I were unable to see. Some were swimming alone, others clinging to life rafts. Realizing the unknown survivors were in immediate danger, Lieutenant Gwinn broke radio silence, declaring, "Ducks on the pond!"[1] He then radioed headquarters on Peleliu and reported

SIGHTED 30 SURVIVORS 011–30 NORTH 133–30 EAST.[2]

Meanwhile, down below, no sooner had my depleted supply of adrenalin died down from the little fish incident, than it shot

114

back up again in an exhilarating rush. I heard a plane! Not one flying at thirty-thousand feet. This one was much lower. My eyes scanned the horizon. The sound seemed to be coming from every direction, making visual contact difficult. My heart pounded inside my chest. I yelled over at McKissick, "I hear a plane!" He yelled back, "So do I!" I thought to myself, *Is this what we've been waiting for? Are our prayers answered?* Suddenly we spotted Gwinn's bomber. And yes, it was much lower than expected. And it was flying on a course directly over us.

Oblivious to our fatigue, we began screaming around our enlarged tongues. Splashing, waving, praying, "O God, please let it be! Please let him see us!" My mind raced with thoughts of, *Will he see us? Can he see us?* As the plane got within about a quarter of a mile, it suddenly took a dive and came right at us within a few hundred feet. We had been spotted! The plane circled over us a couple of times at a very low altitude, then climbed and circled us a few more times. We noticed the plane had wheels on it, making it impossible to land on the water. But we were confident the pilot would radio for help. Suddenly he dove again and circled us at a much slower speed. Then he severely banked the plane and dropped us a life raft. He tilted his wings a couple of times as if to say, "Hang on! We see you!" Then he rose up above us and continued circling.

Lieutenant Gwinn had no idea who we were, but as he flew over us, he began to see many others. He estimated that there were four groups scattered over a seventy-five-mile area. The first group he believed consisted of about thirty; a second group about six miles away consisting of another forty; a third group about two miles from the second with perhaps as many as seventy-five; and a fourth group close by the third that consisted of about thirty-five. Gwinn's radio announcement was the first unwitting report of the USS *Indianapolis* disaster, and later proved to be a key piece of information in solving the puzzle of the *Indy*'s second non-arrival report received at the naval operations base on the island of Leyte.[3]

As he circled us, Gwinn returned to the antenna problem, but this time was able to solve it quickly by reeling in the wire and affixing a rubber hose to it. He then sent a second message:

SEND RESCUE SHIP 11–54 N 133–47 E 150 SURVIVORS IN LIFEBOAT AND JACKETS[4]

While Gwinn surveyed the area, McKissick slowly made his way to the raft that had been dropped within a hundred yards or so from him. In order to swim, I had to once again put on my water-logged jacket and fight the swells and the wind that had picked up significantly and was blowing the raft away from us. As I fought my way to the raft, I remember passing by the deceased sailor that had floated along with us all day. I paused momentarily to say a final farewell. Within a couple hours after reaching the raft, another plane arrived on the scene. To my great relief, this one was a PBY, so it was capable of landing on water.

Gwinn's urgent plea for help had set into motion a rescue effort led by Lt. Adrian Marks, who piloted a PBY-5A Catalina. The amphibious aircraft, used for hunting subs and rescuing downed pilots, reached us at 3:20 p.m. Marks circled over a large area, dropping numerous kinds of provisions. That's when I realized there must be other survivors than just McKissick and myself. Marks later indicated that as he circled over the men at about twenty-five to thirty feet, he could look into the emerald sea and detect hundreds of sharks swimming about. In fact, it was reported that just before Lieutenant Gwinn arrived, an estimated thirty sharks had attacked approximately sixty boys clinging to a floater net, devouring them in a fifteen-minute feeding frenzy.[5]

Impossible Odds

When you hear about the antenna problem that led to Lieutenant Gwinn's discovery of the survivors, it indeed sounds fortunate, even surprising. But it's much, much more than that. Once you begin to calculate the odds of our being discovered by "chance," you realize there is no word to describe it other than *miraculous*.

Many years later at a survivor reunion, Lieutenant Marks helped explain the odds.[6] Begin by picturing a pilot in a cockpit, looking out over the ocean surface. The typical pilot would have been flying at around 10,000 feet and looking down at an angle of about 30 degrees (a pilot almost never looks straight down on the water). In other words, he would be looking down at an angle into water that was four miles in front of him. From this distance, he would be able to see a span of water about five miles wide, catching about twenty square miles at a glance. Keep in mind that Gwinn wasn't looking for the survivors—he didn't even know they were missing. No one did.

In air-sea rescue training missions, the fact that you cannot find a lone swimmer in the ocean is a given. It's just unthinkable. They can only be seen if they have something that makes them more visible, such as a mirror to catch the sunlight to flash in a pilot's eye, or some dye marker that creates a huge colorful spot on the water. Yellow life rafts sometimes work as well, but often they're indistinguishable from cardboard boxes drifting with the current. The *Indy* survivors had none of this. We wore gray life jackets that blended perfectly into the color of the waves.

117

On the fourth day, a boy from Oklahoma saw the sharks eat his best friend. I suppose it was more than his brain could stand. He took his knife, placed it in his mouth (like Tarzan did in the movies), and started chasing sharks. They would stay just far enough ahead of him that he couldn't touch them. He would go under for long periods, making us wonder whether he would come up. I don't know how long this went on, but sometime later, I noticed he wasn't around.

Survivor Sherman C. Booth

An average head is about nine inches tall and six inches wide. Seeing a head that size floating among the waves from four miles away (the typical pilot's vantage point) would be akin to looking at the endwise cross section of a human hair from across the room.

To put it another way, a nautical mile is about 6,080 feet long. A square mile, then, contains 36,966,400 square feet. Remember the twenty-square-mile glance that a pilot sees? That glance contains three-fourths of a billion square feet. And any one human's head floating in the water takes up less than a single square foot. You just don't notice such a thing amid waves and whitecaps. The *only* way one would see anything unusual at all would be to fly much lower and look directly down at the water. Even then, you'd have to be very observant to catch anything unusual happening in the water below. And why would a pilot ever be looking straight down if he or she wasn't looking for something specific?

But wait, there are more astronomical odds: What are the chances of a plane flying over that exact spot at all? First, keep in mind that Gwinn and other search planes were looking for enemy planes and ships, *not* the USS *Indianapolis* survivors in the ocean below. They just happened to be searching that spot of the ocean at the time. Search missions typically went out six hundred miles, and their crews were supposed to watch ten miles on each side of the plane, which means together they would be spanning a six-hundred-mile by twenty-mile area, for a total of 12,000 square miles. That seems like a lot . . . until you consider that the Pacific Ocean is 63,780,000 square miles.

So then, what were the chances Lieutenant Gwinn would fly directly over the survivors? And what were the chances his antenna would lead to him looking straight down on the water at just the right time? It's impossible to calculate.

As Lieutenant Marks, the second pilot to reach us, later told me and other survivors, "I know that most of you prayed a lot; and I know that some of you feel that it made a difference. Wilbur Gwinn is a wonderful man and a fine pilot. He never said that he heard a voice speak to him; but was there an unseen hand upon his shoulder? Did he find you by pure chance? The odds against it are one in a million—nay, one in a billion. But somehow he was chosen as the instrument to overcome these impossible, astronomical odds. Wilbur Gwinn looked down at the split second that would become one of the great moments of history. I, as well as you, am proud to know him as a friend."[7]

I agree. Our rescue was a marvel. And this doesn't even get into the fact that it is not humanly possible for a person to swim for four and a half days with next to no food or water. Not to mention swarmed by hungry sharks. Our survival truly defies reason.

But I would also hasten to add that my survival, along with that of my comrades, was not the ultimate purpose in such a supernatural event. No, whenever God performs any feat that arouses the awe and wonder of His creation, He does so primarily to bear witness to His own glory. And it is to that end I remain committed, for indeed, such a story has no human explanation. Only a sovereign, omnipotent God could have orchestrated such a scenario, for our good and His glory.

Open-Sea Landing

The rescue attempt of Lieutenant Marks and his crew aboard the PBY would prove a tremendous act of heroism. The waves and wind were so fierce that afternoon that such an attempt was borderline suicidal. Yet I believe God compelled them to abandon their natural instinct for self-preservation to do His bidding by bravely landing that large craft in the open sea to bring us to safety.

Marks, knowing that speed was crucial to saving as many lives as possible, decided to ignore normal communication protocol. He sent an uncoded message to Peleliu:

BETWEEN 100 AND 200 SURVIVORS AT POSITION REPORTED [X] NEED ALL SURVIVAL EQUIPMENT AVAILABLE WHILE DAYLIGHT HOLDS [X] SURVIVORS MANY WITHOUT RAFTS

Later in the same message he boldly stated that he would attempt an open-sea landing. This was something he had never tried before, and it was extremely dangerous. In fact, all his squadron's previous attempts had failed to the point that they were expressly prohibited from making such landings.

Marks yelled through his headset at his crew to make sure they were on board with such a decision, and they gave him a thumbs-up. They were going in. Cutting the throttle, he lifted the *Playmate 2*'s nose to set her down in what is called a power stall. The lumbering Catalina hit the top of the first wave, knocking it fifteen feet skyward, then came down on the water even harder than before. They were sure the plane would blow apart at any moment. On the third landing attempt, Marks recalled she "settled down like a hen over an egg." Still, the propellers continued spinning, and there was concern that they might dig into the water and cause the plane to flip over.

Meanwhile, the crew could hear seams and rivets pop; as seawater streamed in, the crew did their best to seal up holes in the plane's skin with cotton and pencils. The radioman had to bail water right away as his compartment in the middle of the plane was quickly filling, and all the crew joined him at a pace of ten to twelve buckets an hour.

Ensign Irving Lefkovitz was Marks's copilot. He took on the task of preparing for rescue even as Marks was determining where, exactly, to steer the plane. It continued to pitch up and down on the large waves as it floated on the ocean's surface.[8]

By the time I reached the raft that Lieutenant Gwinn had dropped for us, McKissick was gone. He had forsaken it and was already swimming toward the PBY that had landed several hundred yards away. Although I could not see the plane, I could hear it. When I reached the deserted raft, it was upside-down. I immediately turned it over and examined it to see if it had any drinking water on it. Finding nothing, I discovered an even greater setback. Due to a large hole, the raft could not be inflated. Then I understood why McKissick had abandoned it. In my frustration, I nearly stayed too long trying to make the raft usable.

By now McKissick was out of sight, headed for the rescue plane. I was sure that he would tell them there was another

Marine out there with him. As I quickly paddled my way toward the sound of the engines, I could tell the plane was not stationary. It was slowly navigating its way through the valleys between the swells. I later learned that Marks was carefully trying to avoid contacting the massive walls of water with his wings while at the same time making his way toward possible survivors.

Marks later described his dangerous maneuverings to the survivors, telling of the heartbreaking decisions they had to make. The crew realized early on that they couldn't rescue everyone. As they were flying overhead, they had noticed that most of the men clung to each other in groups of ten or more, but there were others who were isolated—some dead but most seemingly alive—floating by themselves in their life jackets and were easy targets for sharks. They decided the isolated men were at the greatest risk since they had no one to look after them or even supply moral support and encouragement. They were the ones likely to die in the night. (Keep in mind that he had no idea at that time that all the men had already survived four days in the water.) With all that in mind, they decided to go after the individual swimmers and leave the groups for other rescue planes and boats that were to come soon.[9]

What this meant was that I was one of the first to be rescued. Had I not been previously separated from my group, there is a strong possibility that I would not have been pulled out of the water that afternoon and would have had to wait until the next day when more help arrived. Such a prospect causes me to once again be awed by the unseen hand of divine providence that summoned me away from the group so I could later be among the first rescued. I'm sure I would not have survived another night.

Lieutenant Marks described the horrific pathos of the rescue process, indicating that men would wave and cheer as they saw him slowly taxi toward them. The crew would enthusiastically wave back in recognition, and then deliberately pass them by to pick up the lone stragglers. Marks later lamented, "It was simply incomprehensible. They shouted and shook their fists and wept tears of black despair. And although they knew that they had been seen, the airplane never returned, and they were left to shiver through yet a fifth night until near morning when the USS *Doyle* finally found them."[10]

Eventually I saw the plane. With inexpressible joy I watched it come closer and closer. I had been spotted. I can still see the big wings of that PBY towering over me and hear the deafening sound of the massive engines turning the propellers. Before I knew it, someone pitched me a life ring on a rope. I grabbed hold of the ring but could barely hang on, weighed down by my water-logged jacket. I frantically tried to release my kapok to get a better grip on the ring. It felt as though they were going to pull me in half as they reeled me toward the plane while it was still moving. I was finally able to break the strings that tied my jacket together and slip it off. Once they pulled me up close to the plane, someone grabbed me and heaved me on board. Unable to stand, the crewmen lifted me and carried me inside the plane. Being too weak to sit erect, they stacked me like a sack of feed up against the wall next to other wet and shivering survivors. It was obvious that we were all in the same condition. Covered with a filthy, greasy coat of oil, we all huddled together in a state that I can only describe as being somewhere between life and death. Warmed only by the body heat of unknown comrades, we were now united together by the inseparable bonds of combat survival.

I was happy to be alive but too close to death to really appreciate what had just happened. I wasn't sure if I was dreaming

> Another raft was dropped, and I started to swim after it. Soon I
> was out of gas and just quit swimming. At that moment I heard a
> voice scream, "Grab the ring, grab the ring!" I found the life ring
> in front of me, and was pulled aboard Captain Adrian Marks's PBY.
> I was a SURVIVOR!
>
> Survivor Edward J. Brown

or if it was real. Hardly anyone was talking; our tongues were
swollen from dehydration and our bodies were fatigued beyond
description. As God would have it, I looked across from me and
to my astonishment, the first person I recognized was my buddy
Spooner. I saw his blond hair covered with oil and two protruding
eyes that looked like massive sores of crimson red. Naturally, he
could hardly see anything, much less recognize me. One of the
crewmen had given him a can of green beans and he was using
his hands to feel for some kind of sharp object on the deck of
the aircraft that he could use to open his precious container. I
watched him for a few seconds, and suddenly he located a stud
on the floor and began hacking away at it with the can, trying to
knock a hole in it. Eventually he was successful and turned it up
and began to drink the bean juice. I said to him, "Hey, Marine.
How about sharing some of that with me?" At first he "politely"
told me to leave him alone. But when I told me who I was, he
lunged at me with a frenzied determination to share his prize.

As we embraced in that joyful reunion, I thanked God for
bringing to fulfillment my words to Spooner when earlier I had
said, "Spooner, listen to me. There are only two Marines left in
this group and when everyone else is gone, I'm still going to be

here and you're going to be with me. I know in my heart that God is going to deliver us and we are going to survive this together."

Given my condition, combined with my limited ability to see what was going on aboard the plane, I can only relate a very narrow perspective of what actually happened over the next few hours. But Lieutenant Marks has given beautiful and detailed accounts of how the survivors were cared for and how everyone treated one another.

Playmate 2 carried four water breakers, each holding four and a half gallons of fresh water. This was not nearly enough for so many dehydrated men. In fact, the plane took so many survivors on board that each man could be given just a little over a quart. As soon as each survivor was pulled aboard, they received their first half cup of water. It would take three or four minutes for their stomach to settle, and then they were given half a cup more. Marks guessed that some of the first men aboard probably got a little more than their fair share, but usually after these first two drinks the survivors would fall into a deep sleep. When they awoke, they'd cry out for more.

The hull of the aircraft soon was filled to capacity with two men in each bunk. The airplane crew tried to have the survivors sit upright, but they would collapse and pile up on the floor, two or three deep in every section of the plane. It was no longer at all possible to walk through the plane, and yet every few minutes another survivor—exhausted and sick—was brought aboard.

Marks eventually turned the engines off and they used the wings as extra space for the survivors. This was not easy, since the plane was bobbing up and down on the waves and the men were too weak to help themselves into position on the wings. But this was the only space left, and they couldn't bear not to use every bit of room available. What added to the difficulty was that the wings slanted downward, from front to back, so the men had to be attached with the lines from parachutes lest they slide off into the sea.

That night, *Playmate 2* dropped a sea anchor and drifted. Marks had hoped to continue the rescue after dark with landing lights and an aldis lamp, but he found it impossible. A little more drinking water was found in the radio compartment. They put it in a kettle and someone worked his way up and down each wing, giving the survivors another half a cup. Since the kettle held only so much water, they had to take several trips out and back on the wings, and each time they had to figure out where they'd left off. Remarkably, each time they repeated the process, one dehydrated, exhausted survivor after another would announce, "I've had mine," letting the opportunity for more pass by. It turned out there was enough extra water that night for everyone to have two rations. In spite of their need, not one of the survivors asked for more than their fair share.[11]

In total, Marks had picked up fifty-six survivors that afternoon. As I lay there in that wet and slimy pile of quivering humanity, the comfort of a kept promise brought solace to my soul like a warm fire on a winter night. I knew that as surely as I was alive, God had been faithful to that which He had assured me when I first stepped into the black waters that first night. By the mercies of God, the darkness of that fifth night was vastly different from the four before. This night brought with it hope, not despair. Although my mind drifted in and out of a state of awareness, I do remember an overwhelming sense of worship and praise that flowed from the depths of my soul. My heart echoed the psalmist's words: "I will sing of thy power; yea, I will sing aloud of thy mercy in the morning: for thou hast been my defense and refuge in the day of my trouble" (Psalm 59:16 KJV).

A Beacon of Hope

While nestled among my wet and shivering shipmates, clinging to life in the darkness, I remember seeing the dim glow outside the plane. At first I didn't give it much thought, too weary to even care. But after a while the light grew brighter. Then someone—probably one of the crewmen—announced that the light coming through the doorway was emanating from the destroyer USS *Doyle*, which was slowly but surely coming to get us. Knowing this, that glow took on a new dimension. Its rays beamed a light of hope that pierced the cold darkness of death. Speaking to survivors some years later, Lieutenant Marks poignantly described this fascinating phenomenon that occurred over the four to five hours we quietly waited as the *Doyle* made its way to us:

> In an operation where so many things went wrong, where so many people didn't get the word, and where many of those who did get it failed to appreciate the situation, the perception of Lt. Cdr. W. Graham Claytor in command of the *Doyle* was a shining exception. [12]

Claytor was over one hundred miles away from the survivors when he intercepted a radio conversation between Marks and a search plane. He had already been warned about the possibility of enemy submarines in the area—Marks himself had told him this—but he realized men's lives were hanging by a thread. Survivors were still floating in the water among sharks and their own dead comrades for another night, and he didn't want any more of them to die. If there was something—anything—he could do to help them hold on, he would.

It was a moonless and cloudy night with no stars visible. The wind was cold in spite of our latitude. In the hull and on the wings of Marks's aircraft, men were crying softly from thirst

My greatest jubilation came after dark. We could see a great beam of light that appeared to come down from heaven. I for one am convinced it came from God, although it came to us from the first ship to arrive on the scene. I am forever grateful to the men of the USS *Doyle*.

Survivor William R. Akines

and pain. You have no idea what light can mean under those circumstances; it was hope and courage to the survivors on board. We laid back and stared at that light, summoning up the last bit of courage and strength we had to make it until dawn.

Indeed, that light was a profound encouragement to us all. Certainly for me, and I'm sure for many others, it was just one more reminder of the goodness of God. What a marvelous illustration of the Holy Spirit's words through the apostle James who reminds us that "every good gift and every perfect gift is from above, and cometh down from the Father of lights, with whom is no variableness, neither shadow of turning" (James 1:17 KJV).

Words cannot describe those final hours of deliverance from out of the depths of the vast Pacific. I suppose the most profound realities of life are best expressed with complete silence. In fact, it took me over five years before I would even talk about the ordeal. It was simply too painful, yet also too sacred to mention. Even to this day I can only bring myself to tell the story as a testimony to the glory and goodness of God.

Why are the nations in an uproar and
the peoples devising a vain thing?
The kings of the earth take their stand and
the rulers take counsel together against the
LORD and against His Anointed, saying,
"Let us tear their fetters apart and cast
away their cords from us!"
He who sits in the heavens laughs,
the Lord scoffs at them.
Then He will speak to them in His anger
and terrify them in His fury, saying,
"But as for Me, I have installed My King
upon Zion, My holy mountain. . . ."
Now therefore, O kings, show discernment;
Take warning, O judges of the earth.
Worship the LORD with reverence
and rejoice with trembling.
Do homage to the Son, that He not become angry,
and you perish in the way, for His
wrath may soon be kindled.
How blessed are all who take refuge in Him!

Psalm 2:1–6, 10–12

SEVEN

Tragedy and Triumph— the Fifth Day

It was now getting close to midnight on Friday, August 3—ninety-six hours after our ship had been sunk. The seas continued to churn while fifty-six survivors hung on for life aboard the disabled PBY. I had no idea how many other men were scattered for miles all around us, still clinging to life. With a mesmerizing rhythm, the billows swayed us back and forth under the clouds still glowing by the illumination of the approaching *Doyle*. There was great comfort in knowing the massive destroyer was steadily forging ahead to our rescue. It finally arrived on the scene at 11:45 p.m., some five hours after we were initially picked up. Over the next several hours we were transferred to the *Doyle* from the damaged *Playmate 2*. At 12:30 a.m., the *Doyle* radioed the commander of the Western Carolines:

HAVE ARRIVED AREA [X] AM PICKING UP SURVIVORS FROM THE USS INDIANAPOLIS (CA 35), TORPEDOED AND SUNK LAST SUNDAY NIGHT.[1]

I don't remember too much about the transfer, but I do recall a net being rolled over the side for us to climb up, even though most were unable to do so. I vaguely remember being placed into a motor whaleboat that took a group of us to the ship. They fastened me into a wire basket of some sort and hoisted me aboard ship. After transferring our group of fifty-six, the *Doyle* picked up another thirty-seven survivors that night for a total of ninety-three. By early dawn, their portion of the rescue was complete. Other ships gradually came, finding more sailors strewn over many miles. The following is a list of all the rescue ships that came to the scene on Friday, August 3.[2]

Ship Name	Arrival Time	Rescued
USS *Doyle* DE 368	0015	93
USS *Bassett* APD 73	0052	152
USS *Register* APD 92	0200	12
USS *Dufilho* DE 423	0300	1
USS *Talbot* DE 390	0500	24
USS *Ringness* APD 100	1025	39

As the sun broke through the clouds that morning, the *Doyle* trained its guns on the crippled PBY and sent it to the bottom of the sea. It had been damaged severely in the landing, taking on a lot of water and leaking oil. By noon we were on our way to Peleliu, located five hundred miles from the Philippines and about the same distance from New Guinea, an island that we had earlier taken from the Japanese. It was there that we lost over ten thousand Marines, and the Japanese lost an entire garrison of over 10,500 soldiers.

As we were being rescued, the B-29 crew of the *Enola Gay* was anxiously waiting for the skies to clear over their base on Tinian so they could accomplish their mission. Their predetermined target was Hiroshima. I later learned that on the same day we were rescued, President Truman was returning to the United States from the Potsdam conference where he had met with Great Britain and Russia to strategize the final invasion plans to defeat Japan. While en route from London aboard the cruiser *Augusta*, he confidently informed reporters that America possessed a new weapon that could ultimately end the war. Obviously, the president was right.[3]

As I was taken aboard the *Doyle*, I recall two sailors wrapping my arms around their necks and literally dragging me to a compartment below deck. My legs simply had no strength to hold me. Many of my shipmates were also in critical condition. Some had broken legs and arms, and many suffered excruciating pain from infected shark bites. They stretched me out on some kind of table, removed my clothes, and began gently scrubbing the layers of oil off my skin with kerosene. Next they washed me with a saltwater soap, being extremely careful of the body areas that had rubbed together, producing saltwater ulcers. All of my skin was basically decomposing and would peel off and bleed with the least bit of scrubbing. In the days to come, this proved to be a serious and miserable condition for all the survivors.

After I was cleaned up, my sympathetic attendants dressed me in a set of navy skivvies and placed me in one of the sailor's bunks. Another corpsman brought me some sugared water in a cup, but allowed me to sip only two or three tablespoons at a time.

After the *Doyle* dropped us off at Peleliu for about two days of medical attention, we were transferred aboard the hospital ship USS *Tranquility* on Monday morning, August 6. By about

> One of my raftmates was preparing to amputate my lower leg to prevent gangrene, but we were rescued before any impromptu surgery had to be performed. My group was a handful of sailors picked up by the USS *Register*. My leg was saved.
>
> Survivor Albert Ferguson

1:00 p.m. we were on our way to the Naval Base Hospital 18 on Guam, arriving there on August 8. There they treated us for the painful saltwater ulcers among many with other injuries. I vividly remember how they stretched out my arms and legs and cleaned off the infections—without any anesthetic. Not having any better treatment, they wrapped the ulcers in Vaseline gauze and strapped my limbs to the bed so I could not move. I was required to stay in this position for several days.

Like many others, I had a boil that was bothering me. Mine was in my right armpit. The corpsman said it would eventually need to be lanced. After a few days they stretched me out on a table, then handed me a small bag of ice to hold in my armpit. This was my only anesthesia. I knew I was in trouble when four sailors were brought in to pin my shoulders and legs to the table while the corpsman lanced the boil. Even in my weakened condition, the pain was so excruciating that my adrenaline kicked into full force, making it difficult for the sailors to hold me down. Worse yet, they discovered the boil wasn't ready, so they opened up the incision and stuffed it with Vaseline gauze so it could drain, a procedure that had to be repeated every day for about a week.

It was soon after arriving at the hospital in Guam that I had a visitor, one whom I had seen many times walking topside on the

Survivors en route to the base hospital on Peleliu. (U.S. Navy photograph, National Archives)

forward deck aboard the *Indianapolis*. It was Adm. Raymond Spruance. He had come to my bedside to pin a Purple Heart on my pajama top, then he thanked me for my service, wished me a good recovery, and shook my hand, and moved on to the next survivor. I was deeply moved by his sincerity and honored by his presence. Little did I know that that would be the extent of our recognition until the year 2001.

Shocking News

On August 6, while still in Peleliu aboard the *Tranquility*, a momentous event took place that would forever change the world. While the providence of God was saving our lives, many other lives would be taken on that historic day. For it was on that day that the clouds over Tinian cleared and the *Enola Gay* finally departed with the *Indy*'s top-secret cargo secured in its bomb bay. Unknown to us, at 8:15 a.m., the first atomic bomb (nicknamed "Little Boy") was released over Hiroshima, instantly killing more than 118,000 Japanese and injuring another 140,000, who would ultimately die by the end of the year as a result of the explosion.

On Thursday, August 9, the second atomic bomb was dropped on Nagasaki. This one, nicknamed "Fat Man," was responsible for killing 40,000 Japanese and seriously wounding another 60,000. The *Indianapolis* survivors knew nothing of what had happened.

The news of the detonation of the atomic bombs was finally revealed to us on August 10. It was then that we were able to put it all together. To our utter astonishment, we learned that the top-secret cargo we delivered to Tinian was the crucial components for the two bombs dropped at Hiroshima and Nagasaki. Obviously, the news media was buzzing around everywhere trying to get a special scoop on the story. I was interviewed by a reporter from the *Louisville Times*. I remember it well because I was still secured to my bunk, one of six Kentuckians who had survived. I still have the article, dated August 15, 1945.

On the same day that "Fat Man" was dropped on Japan, Admiral Nimitz called from his headquarters, just a few buildings from where we were recuperating, for a court of inquiry to be opened concerning the sinking of the USS *Indianapolis*. Our loved ones did not know that we had been shipwrecked and rescued. It was the middle of August when we learned that the Navy had waited two weeks after the sinking of the *Indianapolis* to make their first public announcement of the tragedy. Although we did not know it at the time, a cover-up was in the making, and it took time to strategize a response that would stand up to both public and naval scrutiny in the days to come. This would ultimately be proven some fifty years later.

After about two weeks in the hospital, all the survivors were taken to a submarine camp to further convalesce. This was our first opportunity to get together since the rescue. For several days we all discussed the horrors we had experienced and mourned the loss of our shipmates who were not so fortunate. I was shocked when I discovered that only nine of my thirty-nine Marine companions aboard ship had survived. One of my most cherished possessions is a picture of all my fellow Marines under the massive barrels of number 1 turret, with their signatures on the back of the picture.

It was a bittersweet reunion when I met with the other eight Marine survivors. I had seen some of them earlier while recuperating in sick bay, but now we were all together and able to discuss what had happened. In disbelief and with great sympathy, we talked about the thirty who perished, and tried to determine if anyone had been in their group at sea. Each of us had special buddies that we inquired about. We learned that Captain Parke was so involved in swimming around his group—trying to keep them all together and defending them from the sharks—that

> Only twelve survived in our group. There were sixteen of us when they dropped the life rafts, but four died before they picked us up. By that time, I was nothing but pus. My skin had blistered, and I had gone from 130 pounds to 80.
>
> Survivor Verlin L. Fortin

he died of exhaustion. They said that his head finally collapsed into the water, never to rise again.

Our first sergeant, Jacob Greenwald, was not a swimmer but said he got a lot of help, even a spare life jacket, thanks to the help of another Marine survivor, Pvt. Earl Riggins. He indicated that Earl had tied him to the center of the floater net to keep him safe. Everyone had stories that were unique to his group, both in how they survived the ordeal and with vivid details of those who didn't.

Years later, my Marine buddy Miles Spooner gave an interview to a newspaper and described me as "a 'hard-shell' Christian, (who) quoted Bible verses, prayed, and pleaded with God during their extended time afloat."

> "I didn't care much for religion then," Spooner said, but he's changed his mind over the years. Did religion save him and Harrell? "Probably so," he said, in a choked voice.[4]

I am thankful that the Lord gave me a steadfast hope and a desire to pray to Him during such an agonizing ordeal. But make no mistake; it was the God of the Bible, not mere religion, that saved us.

We later learned of the gruesome recovery effort conducted on August 4 through August 9 by four reconnaissance ships: the destroyers *Helm* (DD 388) and *Aylwin* (DD 355), and the destroyer escorts *French* (DE 367) and *Alvin C. Cockrell* (DE 366). After searching for hundreds of miles, they retrieved a total of ninety-one bodies for identification and burial.

The tragedy and insanity of war is well illustrated in the report that was drafted by the *Helm*. The report stated that most of the bodies were entirely naked, although a few had shirts on.

Nine Marine survivors of the USS *Indianapolis*. Top row (left to right): Miles Spooner, Earl Riggins, Paul Uffelman, Giles McCoy, Melvin Jacob. Bottom row (left to right): Max Hughes, Raymond Rich, Jacob Greenwald, and me, Edgar Harrell (1945).

There was no way to recognize their faces because they were all so horribly bloated and decomposed from their time in the water. Half of the bodies had been attacked by sharks; some were closer to skeletons than corpses. The rescue mission witnessed sharks attacking bodies and had to drive them off with rifle fire.

> Identifying the bodies was extremely difficult. The skin had come off of most of the hands, either from decomposition or sharks, so getting fingerprints was usually out of the question. If there was skin left on the hands, sometimes the Medical Officer could dehydrate it and attempt to take prints. But most identification had to come from personal effects, if at all. Projectiles were used to sink the bodies after they'd been examined.[5]

An acquaintance of mine, Dr. John Neumann, who was a member of the USS *Helm*, had charge of a burial detail of the men of the USS *Indianapolis*. Ironically, Neumann's most frightening experience with war and death occurred after the war officially ended. He was among the Navy physicians called to recover the survivors and the floating dead after the sinking.

> I thought I had seen the worst, but it wasn't anything like recovering the bodies from the *Indianapolis*. As we prepared the dead for burial at sea, I saw so many dead sailors and Marines gutted apart. It was obvious that a shark had ripped off an arm or leg. The stench and the condition of the survivors as well as the dead was very dreadful. Some of our [medical] team just couldn't take it and had to be replaced.[6]

The process of mourning was difficult for each of us. On the one hand, our hearts were filled with joy because we had survived; on the other hand, we felt twinges of guilt because we had not met the same fate as our comrades. Competing emotions were only complicated by the difficulties of our own physical and psychological wounds—some far deeper than we could have imagined—wounds that would fester for the rest of our lives.

Catastrophic Reflections

Our minds also reflected upon the inconceivable catastrophe caused by the bombs we had delivered. While no one rejoiced in such a calamity, we understood then, as we do now, that the devastation produced by the atomic bombs was merciful in comparison to the ongoing fire bombings that continued to incinerate the Japanese on a daily basis. One account indicates that in one night, 325 bombers destroyed sixteen square miles of

Tokyo, killing 100,000 men, women, and children and injuring untold thousands more.[7]

Relating a conversation he had with his pilot, one B-29 navigator named Tom Banks described what he saw firsthand during the summer of 1945:

> "Pilot to Navigator, over."
>
> "How far are we from the Japanese coast?"
>
> "About ninety nautical miles."
>
> "Better recheck, Navigator. We must be closer than that. Come up front and look."
>
> As I knelt between the pilot and the copilot, the pilot described an arc with his finger from far to the left to far to his right. The earth was on fire. No one spoke, I finally managed to mumble, "We're still ninety miles away."
>
> As we approached the Japanese mainland, we could see that hell had been made real on the face of the earth. [8]

Everything Banks saw was so consumed by fire that nothing was distinguishable—plants, stores, houses, people. There was nothing visible to bomb, so his pilot ordered him to just pick a spot and drop their payload.

The religious fanaticism of the Japanese predisposed them to willingly die for their emperor—an inevitable reality had the war

> I have often felt that I had a unique Navy experience, being from Indiana and ending up on the USS *Indianapolis*. I participated in eight of the ten operations, the last being Okinawa. I am proud to have been a member of the crew that delivered the atomic bomb.
>
> Survivor Donald L. Beaty

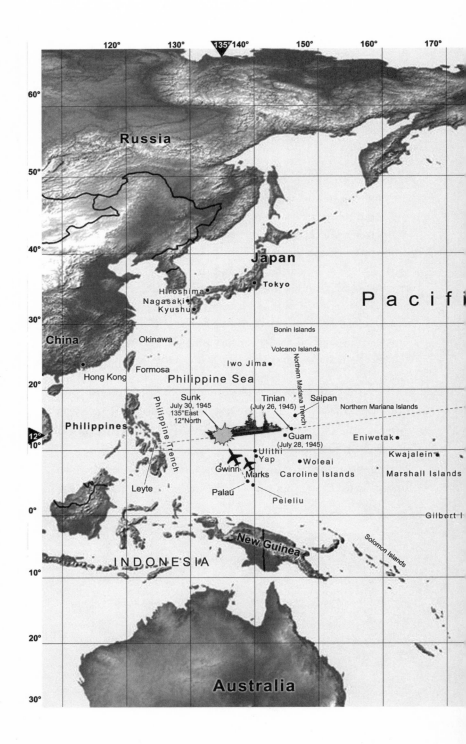

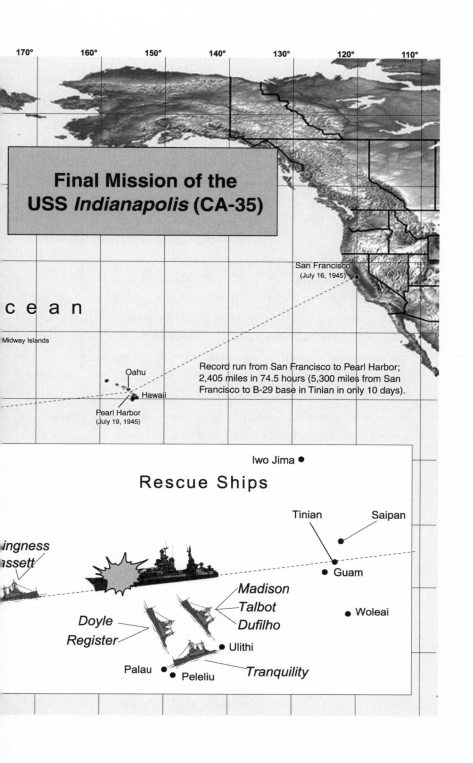

Final Mission of the USS *Indianapolis* (CA-35)

170° 160° 150° 140° 130° 120° 110°

c e a n

Midway Islands

San Francisco
(July 16, 1945)

Oahu

Hawaii

Pearl Harbor
(July 19, 1945)

Record run from San Francisco to Pearl Harbor;
2,405 miles in 74.5 hours (5,300 miles from San
Francisco to B-29 base in Tinian in only 10 days).

Iwo Jima ●

Rescue Ships

Tinian   Saipan

ingness
assett

Guam

Madison
Talbot
Dufilho

● Woleai

Doyle
Register

Ulithi

Palau ●
● Peleliu

Tranquility

continued. While the death tolls from the atomic bombs were indeed staggering, had they not been dropped, causing Japan to surrender, these numbers would have been multiplied many times by the continuation of the fire bombings alone. But these horrendous bombings pale in significance compared to what the Allies were planning to do next. Their plans for a full-scale military invasion of Japan would have cost far more lives than those lost at Hiroshima and Nagasaki combined.

Top-secret military plans labeled Operation Downfall were later declassified, revealing plans for two massive invasions of Japan. On October 29, 1945, the Fortieth Infantry Division and the 158th Regimental Combat Team would invade and occupy a small island twenty-eight miles south of Kyushu where they would establish seaplane bases and a refuge for American carrier-based aircraft. This would precede an amphibious assault three days later on November 1, code-named Operation Olympic. The British would land 1.5 million combat troops, and the Americans would land 3 million more. A second invasion, Operation Coronet, was scheduled to commence on March 1, 1946, delivering twenty-two combat divisions to destroy approximately one million Japanese committed to defending the island of Honshu and the Tokyo Plain. General Willoughby, the chief of intelligence for General MacArthur, conservatively estimated American casualties to be around one million by the fall of 1946.[9] One could only imagine the loss of life for the British and Japanese.

History records that President Truman had four alternatives for trying to end the war: (1) the use of the atomic bomb, (2) invasion of Japan (a two-phase operation), (3) maintain blockades and continue conventional bombing, or (4) negotiate a peaceful settlement. Obviously, President Truman chose the use of the atomic bomb because he was convinced that it would end the war quickly and save the many hundreds of thousands of U.S. and British lives that would have been lost during the invasion. He also believed that the bomb would be a powerful deterrent to help contain the expansionist agenda of the USSR. Although we can never know for certain, it would certainly appear that he was right on all accounts.

War is an amazing thing, an evil that defies description. Yet I am thankful that God has protected our great nation down through the years from murderous tyrants who have come against us.

Home at Last

The escort carrier *Hollandia* transported all of us from Guam back to San Diego. On September 26, over three hundred survivors of the greatest naval catastrophe at sea arrived on the shores of the country they loved and served, only to be met with a paltry Salvation Army band. I cannot say that we knew what to expect, but we certainly thought there would be a more enthusiastic and official welcome. The rather large crowd on the pier had assembled to welcome home the crew of the *Hollandia* and knew nothing of the *Indianapolis* survivors. To my knowledge, none of our families or friends greeted us. Most did not even know our whereabouts. We remained on land as we were at sea—lost and neglected. We all had a mounting sense that we were somehow an embarrassment to the Navy, though at the time we did not understand why.

With no official welcome, we all came ashore and invisibly made our way through the crowd, somewhat envious of the jubilant and legitimate welcome for their loved ones on the

Hollandia. My eight Marine companions and I looked in vain for an official Marine reception that would at least transport us to the Marine Corp Base. We finally located an MP who helped us find a bus. I relate this story not to elicit sympathy, but only to underscore the realities that caused us all to become increasingly suspicious that something was wrong.

Someone has well said, "Truth and time walk hand in hand." Indeed, over the next few months we began to understand why we experienced such a mysterious cloud of concealment and disregard. The Navy was up to something. And the story of the *Indianapolis* had to stay out of the headlines until they had all their political ducks in a row.

Open thy mouth, judge righteously,
and plead the cause of the poor and needy.

Proverbs 31:9 KJV

CHAPTER

EIGHT

Journey for Justice

While there were other naval vessels sunk as a result of combat during the war, only the *Indianapolis* met her fate while leaving the enemy that sunk her completely unscathed. Worse yet, it was estimated that only one-third of the casualties suffered were a result of the initial attack. The other two-thirds were victims of Navy incompetence—a series of debacles that placed us in harm's way, unescorted and our SOS ignored, forcing hundreds of men to fend for themselves in the open sea. As I mentioned, the disaster is now considered the greatest naval catastrophe at sea in the history of the U.S. Navy.

Because of their radical commitment to avoid culpability, the Navy concealed many facts. Instead, the blame was placed on our skipper. As in most politics, spin and selective reasoning typically exonerate the guilty and indict the innocent. Such was the case with Captain McVay. Unfortunately, the truth would not be fully disclosed to the public for over fifty years, when

Navy documents were finally declassified and various individuals began to come together searching for truth and justice.

On Monday, August 13, 1945, a court of inquiry convened according to Admiral Nimitz's orders. Knowing that news of the sinking would eventually reach the public, and desiring to know the facts, the Navy needed some answers—and they needed them fast. At this point, they were still unclear about how we were sunk. The scuttlebutt even included a rumor that we hit a mine. With so many of the recuperating survivors scattered in Guam, Leyte, Peleliu, and Samar, it was virtually impossible to gather all the facts. Although the inquiry board conceded that they "were starting the proceedings without having available all the necessary data," that did not stop them from convening and asking many pertinent questions. They needed to know what caused the disaster, why there was a delay in rescue, who was at fault, and if there were any violations of military laws.

Out of the 317 men that survived, only the testimonies of Captain McVay, four other officers, and fifteen enlisted men were heard. According to historian Dan Kurzman in his book *Fatal Voyage*, as each witness testified, responsibility was tossed back and forth and down the line. According to the officers of the Philippine Sea Frontier (Commodore Gilletee, Captain Granum, Lieutenant Commander Sancho, and Lieutenant Gibson), U.S. Pacific Command (CINCPAC) was at fault because it had not given any instructions regarding what to do about nonarrivals of combatant ships. Since they were told not to report arrivals, they assumed they should not report nonarrivals either. Meanwhile, Sancho reported that his subordinate, Gibson, failed to tell him the *Indianapolis* was overdue for arrival.

Commodore Carter, who was in charge of CINCPAC, admitted there had been no order given regarding nonarrivals, but it was common sense that they should have been reported by both Gibson and Admiral McCormick. Admiral McCormick, meanwhile, passed the blame back to the Philippine Sea Frontier officers, asking why they hadn't kept track of the *Indy*. According to McCormick, the cable he was supposed to get, letting him know that the *Indianapolis* was now under his command, was decoded incorrectly and never delivered.

Captain Naquin and Lieutenant Waldron of the Marianas

Charles Butler McVay III, captain, USS *Indianapolis*.

Command were questioned as well, even though their commander, Admiral Murray, was one of the judges. Naquin admitted he had information about Japanese submarines in the area and that they'd sunk the *Underhill*, but he still deemed the threat negligible. Waldron said he was uninformed of this sinking. Round and round it went with everyone passing the blame to someone else. No one, it seemed, was responsible.[1]

The Need for a Scapegoat

As the proceedings dragged on, Captain McVay struggled with pessimism. His reputation was at stake, perhaps even his career. Although he had not yet been charged with any dereliction of duty, he knew the Navy would need a scapegoat. Naturally, he feared it would be him. However, as the inquiry drew to a close, McVay declined to make a closing argument. After all, to his surprise and relief, he had not been indicted in any way.

In fact, by the end of the inquiry, he believed that ultimately the Navy's much-needed blame would fall where it rightfully should—squarely on the shoulders of those on shore. Unfortunately, that is not the way things turned out. Again, historian Dan Kurzman recounts the appalling conclusion to the inquiry:

> A court-martial seemed out of the question. America had lost over seven hundred ships in the war, and not one of their skippers had been court-martialed. The judges, no doubt, realized that if they were to single him out, it would be obvious that the Navy was looking for a scapegoat.
>
> McVay thus dared to hope that the velvet-gloved treatment he had so far received at this hearing was a presage of lenience for him, and he was unshaken even when the judge advocate stated unequivocally: "Any officer found negligent should be punished!"
>
> But then, as he sat in the hearing room for the last time, he was shocked to learn that the velvet gloves had an abrasive lining. The judge advocate was piling "fact" upon "fact," building up to a set of "false" conclusions:
>
> - Lieutenant Waldron had warned him of the submarine menace, and yet the captain did not zigzag on the fatal night.
> - Visibility was good on that night, making it even more essential for him to zigzag.
> - He delayed sending out an SOS message.
>
> McVay sat quietly, listening in disbelief. "The judge advocate was wrong on all three counts!" he cried to himself in bitter rage.
>
> Despite his fury and dismay, McVay clung to a straw of optimism as the court began apportioning the blame. It recommended that Lieutenant Gibson be sent a Letter of Admonition, a lesser censure than a reprimand, for failing to report the nonarrival of the *Indianapolis* in Leyte; and that Admiral

McCormick be ordered to discipline his staff for not decoding the cable that explained why the *Indianapolis* would be reporting to him. [2]

Even though McVay felt that Gibson and McCormick were being treated unjustly, as they were given the blame for the misjudgments of their superiors, he also thought this might be a hopeful sign. After all, if the judges believed mistakes were made by people ashore, perhaps he himself would not be held responsible. Perhaps his own career would not be in jeopardy.

This was wishful thinking. The judges recommended that he receive a letter of reprimand and also a general court-martial for "performing his duties inefficiently and endangering lives through his negligence."[3]

Helplessness and Disbelief

The die was now cast for our skipper's fate. As news about the inquiry trickled down to the survivors, we all felt his pain. A strange cloud of disbelief, even betrayal, hovered over us. Suddenly we all had become victims of a profound injustice. It was not just the captain being maligned, but because of our loyalty to him, we all felt attacked. How, after all we had been through, could they possibly come to such a conclusion? Over seven hundred ships had been sunk during the war and not one captain had been court-martialed. We were at a complete loss to understand their reasoning. The same helpless feelings of being adrift at sea began to grip our hearts again as we felt abandoned once more by the Navy and powerless to do anything about it.

As I recuperated in the Marine Corps Base hospital in San Diego, I reflected upon the captain we all so deeply admired. I would often replay the scenes of that horrific night. And every

> Yes, I am mad they didn't pick us up. If you go on leave or liberty and you're ten minutes late, you are court-martialed. But here is a ship, a quarter of a mile long, weighing ten thousand tons, with twelve hundred people . . . the thing is missing for days, and nobody looks for it. I am still bitter about that. I feel sorry for the guys who died. I figured maybe the good Lord had His arm around me.
>
> Survivor James F. Newhall

time I relived those moments, hearing the screams, feeling the explosions, and stepping into the oil-laden water, I could never determine anything that would place blame upon the skipper. It simply made no sense to me, nor to my shipmates. My frustration finally motivated me to write the captain.

December 9, 1945

Dear Captain McVay,

I've been reading about the court-martial they've been trying to pull in Washington, and I must say I think it very absurd. I've read the testimonies given by some of the crew members, and if I can offer any help, I would be more than glad to do so.

I know personally the word was passed orally to abandon ship. Also I believe that as many as nine hundred crewmen left the ship, and the remaining complement were trapped below decks or killed instantly. Most of these were in sick-bay country and in the two compartments below.

I'm now at M.C.B. waiting discharge.

Respectfully yours,
Corp. Edgar Harrell

Captain McVay kindly responded to my offer in the following correspondence:

December 14, 1945

Corp. Edgar A. Harrell
Unit 3 Casual Platoon
R & R Center, M.C.B.
San Diego, California

Dear Harrell:

Thank you very kindly for your letter of December the ninth, which reached me yesterday. I appreciate greatly your offer to testify that you personally heard the order to abandon ship, and should I feel it necessary to call you to Washington, after your offer, I will not hesitate in doing so. Since all the surviving officers and many of the men are now here, I believe that we have enough witnesses to place all the facts before the Court.

There are two of your Detachment here now, McCoy and Rich, but if I need your backing, I will ask them to order you on.

Again, many thanks for your offer.

Very sincerely yours,
Chas. B. McVay, 3rd
Captain, U.S. Navy

As bereaved family members of deceased sailors and Marines learned of the fatal sinking, they demanded answers. It's human nature to look for someone or something to blame when great tragedy strikes. Unfortunately, many families blamed the captain for their loss. At some level this was understandable because they did not have the facts. The hate mail and death threats came pouring in—a most unfortunate burden for the captain to bear.

Trial by General Court-Martial

Captain McVay's trial began on December 3, 1945. The secretary of the Navy, James Forrestal, brought two charges against him. The first—"negligence suffering a vessel of the Navy to be hazarded"—stated,

> In that Charles B. McVay, 3rd, captain, U.S. Navy, while so serving in command of the USS *Indianapolis*, making passage singly, without escort, from Guam, Marianas Islands, to Leyte, Philippine Islands, through an area in which enemy submarines might be encountered, did, during good visibility after moonrise on 29 July 1945, at or about 10:30 p.m., minus nine and one-half zone time, neglect and fail to exercise proper care and attention to the safety of said vessel in that he neglected and failed, then and thereafter, to cause a zigzag course to be steered, and he, the said McVay, through said negligence, did suffer the said USS *Indianapolis* to be hazarded, the United States then being in a state of war.[4]

The second charge against him was "culpable inefficiency in the performance of duty." Specifically stated,

> In that Charles B. McVay, 3rd, captain, U.S. Navy, while so serving in command of the USS *Indianapolis*, making passage from Guam, Marianas, to Leyte, Philippine Islands, having been informed at or about 12:10 a.m., minus nine and one-half zone time, on 30 July 1945, that said vessel was badly damaged and in sinking condition, did then and there fail to issue and see effected such timely orders as were necessary to cause said vessel to be abandoned, as it was his duty to do, by reason of which inefficiency many persons on board perished with the sinking of said vessel, the United States then being in a state of war.[5]

Not only were the charges brought against Captain McVay contrived, the proceedings were also highly unusual, further betraying a hidden agenda. To everyone's astonishment, the Navy ordered Japanese submarine Commander Hashimoto, the man who sunk the *Indy*, to be called from Japan as a witness against the captain. This was unprecedented in the history of the Navy. It was an unconscionable aberration of justice for the United States to place an enemy in a position to accuse one of our own patriots. It is interesting to note, however, that Hashimoto's testimony actually worked in favor of the captain's defense, in that he indicated that it would have made no difference whether the ship was zigzagging or not. Given all the conditions on that fateful night, his torpedoes would have hit the ship regardless.

Ultimately, the Navy found McVay guilty of the first charge—failure to zigzag—and not guilty of the second charge—failure to issue the order to abandon ship. The court sentenced him to lose one hundred numbers in both his temporary rank of captain and in his permanent rank of commander. Interestingly, his final fitness report record read: "This record contains only one unfavorable entry, a Letter of Reprimand concerning the

On that first day our hopes were high about being rescued. Weren't we expected in Leyte? Little did we know no one was looking for us. We just vanished. To this day, I can't believe that an admiral with a staff of a hundred men did not question where his flagship was when it did not arrive. Too much was ignored and forgotten. Why did so many men have to die?

Survivor Victor R. Buckett

loss of the USS *Indianapolis*, but otherwise this record of the accused deserves the rating of outstanding during his entire commissioned service."[6]

The Navy's blunders were now safely concealed in the archives, well hidden from the public's discerning sight. They had sacrificed our skipper on the altar of Navy pride. Personal vengeance also seemed to fuel the injustice against the captain. Evidently, one very influential father, Thomas D'Arcy Brophy, was so grieved over the loss of his son, Tom Brophy, that he set out on a personal crusade to seek revenge upon the man whom he believed was responsible for his son's death—Captain McVay. Testimonies later indicated that Brophy used his formidable political influence to pressure Secretary Forrestal, and even his friend President Truman, to do all they could to destroy McVay.[7]

While the verdict could have been worse, it was, nevertheless, the end of Captain McVay's noble career. In an effort that would now seem to be an attempt to alleviate a guilty conscience, his commendations and awards were also included into the record, namely: "twenty-six years and the Silver Star 'for conspicuous gallantry and intrepidity' in the Solomon Islands campaign, the Bronze Star with combat V for the Okinawa assault, the Purple Heart and the Asiatic-Pacific Campaign Medal with four bronze stars."[8]

Later, in 1946, Secretary Forrestal remitted Captain McVay's sentence and restored him to duty, largely due to the recommendation of Admiral Nimitz who had become Chief of Naval Operations. The good captain then served his remaining time in the New Orleans Naval District, where he retired in 1949 with the rank of Rear Admiral.

The Birth of the Survivors' Organization

During this time, the survivors' conviction of Captain McVay's innocence continued to fester like an unrelenting boil. Our desire to see him completely exonerated gradually took shape over the next several years. In 1958, an editor of the Associated Press and former wartime naval correspondent in the Pacific, Richard F. Newcomb, wrote the first book detailing the sinking, entitled *Abandon Ship!* For the survivors, Newcomb's accounting only added fuel to the fire of vindication as his research gave further clarity to the miscarriage of justice.

During this period, Marine survivor Giles McCoy was also busy writing letters and making phone calls in an effort to contact survivors and organize a reunion as well as a strategy to help exonerate the captain. After a Herculean effort on his part, 220 of the 317 survivors were located and invited to our first reunion on July 30 and 31, 1960, held in Indianapolis, Indiana. Finally, after fifteen years, we were all reunited and organized to once again go into battle for Captain McVay.

In the initial stages of organization, I met with several survivors including McCoy and was asked to be program chairman for the first reunion. One of my responsibilities was to invite Captain McVay to come as our guest of honor and speak to us. He agreed to come, but asked that they not reserve more than fifteen minutes for his talk.

When the long-anticipated day finally arrived, most of the 220 men and their wives gathered together at the airport to greet our dear captain. Approximately five hundred people formed a line in his honor. In shock, he and his wife, Louise, exited the plane and tearfully made their way past the sailors and Marines who stood at full attention, saluting him with tears streaming down their cheeks. It was a grand and glorious sight. He later

I always will have great respect for Captain McVay. I believe he was correct in his decision. If it were possible, I would serve under him again and be very happy to do so.

Survivor Claudus Evans

acknowledged that he was somewhat concerned about how he would be received, given the disgraceful reprimand at the general court-martial. Certainly, with the relentless barrage of hate mail he received from devastated families, he was predisposed to thinking the worst. But to his great joy, he was received with

The airport reception for Captain McVay at our first survivors' reunion. That's me shaking his hand, with my wife, Ola, to my right (1960).

utmost respect and military dignity. After all, we knew he was innocent.

The joy and triumph of our reunion, however, was short lived. In 1961, Captain McVay's faithful wife was diagnosed with cancer and died. A few years later, in 1965, his beloved grandson died. Then, for reasons no one will ever fully know, Capt. Charles B. McVay III became convinced that life was no longer worth living, and in November 1968 he committed suicide.

Justice at Last

The news of the captain's death, though painful, only fanned the flames of our resolve to see him exonerated. Our dedicated chairman of the survivor's organization, Marine Giles McCoy, pressed harder and harder to correct the injustice. By then, several books on the sinking of the *Indianapolis* were in print, each one painting a dark cloud over the Navy and the way it had treated an excellent captain.

Every five years the survivors would have another reunion. And every time we met, we continued in our commitment to push forward at all cost to see him cleared of all blame. We even refused a Navy Presidential Citation as a protest against his mistreatment. Finally, in the providence of God, we began to see a light at the end of this very long tunnel of injustice and political stonewalling.

Hunter Scott, a sixth-grade elementary school student from Pensacola, Florida, had been inspired by the motion picture *Jaws*, in which an actor played the role of a USS *Indianapolis* survivor. Although I have not seen the movie—I avoid anything that reminds me of the horrors we experienced—the "survivor" vividly described our plight in the shark-infested waters.

Intrigued, the young boy wanted to learn more. After conferring with his father, he decided to research the story and enter his findings in a sixth-grade history fair.

In an article that appeared in *Naval History* magazine, Hunter, belying his young age, provided an excellent summary of the evidence he discovered that was instrumental in exonerating Captain McVay. There he wrote,

> After two years of research and interviews with almost all remaining *Indianapolis* survivors, I have amassed what one naval historian has called "the greatest collection of information on the USS *Indianapolis* in the world." On 22 April 1998, accompanied by Congressman Joe Scarborough (R-FL), Congresswoman Julia Carson (D-IN), and 11 *Indianapolis* survivors, I personally dropped H.R. 3710 into the hopper on the floor of Congress. This bill will erase all mention of the court-martial and conviction from the record of Captain Charles B. McVay III and award a Presidential Unit Citation to the USS *Indianapolis* and her crew.[9]

The legislation was passed by Congress and signed by President Clinton. The language concerning Captain McVay read:

> With respect to the sinking of the USS *Indianapolis* (CA-35) on July 30, 1945, and the subsequent court-martial conviction of the ship's commanding officer, Captain Charles Butler McVay III, arising from that sinking, it is the sense of Congress:
>
> (1) in light of the remission by the Secretary of Navy of the sentence of the court-martial and the restoration of Captain McVay to active duty by the Chief of Naval Operations, Fleet Admiral Chester Nimitz, that the American people should now recognize Captain McVay's lack of culpability for the tragic loss of the USS *Indianapolis* and

the lives of the men who died as a result of the sinking of that vessel; and

(2) in light of the fact that certain exculpatory information was not available to the court-martial board and that Captain McVay's conviction resulted therefrom, that Captain McVay's military record should now reflect that he is exonerated for the loss of the USS *Indianapolis* and so many of her crew.[10]

Every survivor with whom I have spoken joins me in applauding the efforts of Hunter Scott and all the other senators, members of Congress, and concerned citizens instrumental in securing justice for our captain and resolution for the men that served him.

Blessed be the God and Father
of our Lord Jesus Christ,
who according to His great mercy has
    caused us to be born again
to a living hope through the resurrec-
    tion of Jesus Christ from the dead,
to obtain an inheritance which is imperish-
    able and undefiled and will not fade away,
reserved in heaven for you, who are pro-
    tected by the power of God
through faith for a salvation ready to
    be revealed in the last time.
In this you greatly rejoice,
even though now for a little while, if necessary,
you have been distressed by various tri-
    als, that the proof of your faith,
being more precious than gold which is perishable,
even though tested by fire,
may be found to result in praise and glory and
    honor at the revelation of Jesus Christ;
and though you have not seen Him, you love Him,
and though you do not see Him now,
but believe in Him,
you greatly rejoice with joy inex-
    pressible and full of glory,
obtaining as the outcome of your faith
    the salvation of your souls.

1 Peter 1:3–9

Epilogue

After our rescue, my hospitalization in Guam, and our arrival in San Diego on October 2, my recovery at the Marine Corps Base did not go smoothly. Two days in, an ambulance had to rush me to Balboa Hospital in San Diego with a perforated appendix. But before they could operate, they had to reduce my elevated white-blood-cell count. I had a life-threatening fever requiring twenty-nine days of penicillin.

Finally, the day for surgery arrived. After giving me a spinal tap, they strapped me down on the operating table and began the surgery. I was not put under and was able to watch the procedure on the overhead monitor. Unable to move my arms, I told the nurse standing by my head that my nose was itching. She quickly addressed the situation with a tissue and a good rubbing. But my relief was short lived, and a few minutes later I had to complain about it again. This time, however, a white-haired gentleman in a white uniform and mask standing near my bed repeated what the nurse had just done. When he was finished, the nurse leaned over and asked me, "Marine, how does it feel to have an admiral rub your nose?" All I could think to say was, "Thank you, sir."

In January of 1946, after spending three months at the hospital in San Diego, I was sent to Great Lakes, Illinois, where I was discharged from the Marine Corps. As it turned out, all the documentation of my promotion to sergeant (two days before the sinking) went down with the ship, so it was never official and I was discharged as a corporal. I then went back home to Murray, Kentucky, and enrolled in college. But the wounds of war were still too fresh, too distracting. More healing needed to take place, more time needed to pass. So after my freshman year I decided to go to work with my father in construction.

In July of 1947, I married Ola Mae Cathey, the same brunette who caught my eye in high school four and a half years earlier. Together we had two children, Cathey and David, and we now have eight grandchildren and eight great-grandchildren.

God didn't stop after blessing me with a wonderful family. He blessed me in the business world as well. In 1950 I became a distributor for the Pella Window Company in Iowa City, Iowa. A year later I transferred to the Quad Cities and established an office in Rock Island, Illinois. There the Lord allowed me to prosper, and I was able to expand my territory into three states. I eventually sold my business in 1985.

During those years I was actively involved in my local church as both a leader and lay teacher. I also served as a trustee for the

> Although all of us experienced a great tragedy, I have never been sorry I joined the United States Navy. Nothing is too great to protect freedom for our country.
>
> Survivor Dale F. Krueger

Ola and me on our 50th wedding anniversary (1997).

Moody Bible Institute for over fifteen years. After retirement I moved to Paris, Tennessee, close to my birthplace, and then in 2006 I moved to Clarksville, Tennessee, where I commute to the church my son, David, pastors near Nashville. I continue to travel all over the country telling my story and giving God the glory for rescuing me not only out of the depths of the ocean, but more important, out of the depths of my sin. All I want is to remain a faithful husband, father, grandfather, and great-grandfather, and to be a testimony of God's transforming and saving grace.

No one can possibly fathom the horrors of war unless they have experienced them firsthand. To be sure, no one can comprehend what that entire generation endured during that hellish Second World War. But we not only survived—somehow we thrived. In his book *The Greatest Generation*, Tom Brokaw says my generation is "the greatest generation any society has ever produced." Whether or not that is true, I know that my generation certainly did not come through it all unscathed. For many, the war didn't end with the Japanese surrender, especially for those who suffered extreme physical and psychological trauma like the survivors of the USS *Indianapolis*. Some of my buddies succumbed to alcoholism, depression, or even suicide.

At first I, like all the others, tried to forget what happened. But certain sights, sounds, and smells would trigger my memory and instantly take me back to places I didn't want to go. I could see suicide planes and the bow cut off the ship, hear explosions and bulkheads breaking, and on and on. It was six months after I got home before I finally acquiesced to the constant queries of a respected friend and allowed myself to talk about what happened. Once I got started, I found that I couldn't stop. Finally, my father tearfully said, "Son, that's enough for now." It was the first any of them had heard about what actually happened, and it was more than they could bear.

Years later while in Hawaii on a business trip, I decided to walk down to the edge of the ocean. But when I got close, I stopped and stared. It was as though I was in a hypnotic trance. As I looked out at the open sea, suddenly I could see myself swimming. I could see sharks, the faces of shipmates, and bloated bodies. I could even hear men screaming. Finally, I realized I had to walk away.

To this day I will not set foot in the ocean. But by God's grace I was gradually able to separate my past from the present and joyfully anticipate the future. I understand more fully what the apostle Paul means when he says, "If you have been raised up with Christ, keep seeking the things above, where Christ is. . . . Set your mind on the things above, not on the things that are on earth. For you have died and your life is hidden with Christ in God" (Colossians 3:1–3).

Lifelong Bonds

There remains a special bond between the survivors and our families even to this day. The fiery crucible of our ordeal at sea has, for many, tempered the steel of our faith in God and forged a powerful sword of patriotism for the country we love. Every other year the survivors and our families and friends meet in July in Indianapolis, Indiana, for a reunion—a wonderful season of fellowship, worship, and memorial.

The USS *Indianapolis* (CA-35) Survivors' Organization designed, erected, and financed the USS *Indianapolis* National Memorial in honor of the ship and her crew. Located at the north end of the Canal Walk in Indianapolis, it was dedicated on August 2, 1995. That same year it was designated a National Memorial by an act of Congress, one of only twenty-six such memorials. It is essentially a beautifully landscaped park open

> I sometimes think that my shipmates who were killed or eaten by sharks were the lucky ones. We who were left have had almost fifty years of mental pain. Dates and faces lose their distinction, but the horror never goes away. The older I get the more it bothers me.
>
> Survivor Cozell L. Smith Jr.

At our 1990 survivors' reunion, I posed with Charles McKissick, the only shipmate still alive from our group when we were rescued, forty-five years earlier.

to the public twenty-four hours a day, seven days a week. A stately monument resembling the *Indianapolis* graces the site, with the names of the ship's company and one passenger who made up her final crew engraved on its south face.

Families, friends, and supporters of the men of the *Indianapolis* have now formed an organization called the Second Watch, dedicated to assist the USS *Indianapolis* Survivors' Organization and to promote citizenship and patriotism in our beloved country. I applaud their efforts. We must continue to remind our children that freedom is not free. And for this reason, many brave men and women have sacrificed their lives for this great nation.

Due to the treacherous terrain and enormous depths in the Philippine Sea where the *Indy* was sunk, recent attempts to locate

Our survivors' organization designed, erected, and financed the USS *Indianapolis* (CA-35) National Memorial in honor of the ship and crew. It was dedicated on August 2, 1995.

the ship have proven futile. After a grueling exploration, the crew of an expeditionary vessel named the *Sea Eagle* concluded that their disappointing search must be abandoned. Consequently,

Five Marine survivors at our 2002 reunion (left to right): Earl Riggins, Jacob Greenwald, Melvin Jacob, me, and Giles McCoy.

173

the passengers, explorers, and a few *Indy* survivors on board conducted a most appropriate and appreciated memorial service. An American flag presented to the *Indianapolis* survivors by Admiral Tom Fellin was draped over a makeshift raft. A simple block of granite was placed on the flag, along with a plaque commemorating the ship and her crew.

After a brief memorial service, the "memorial barge" was solemnly lowered into the water off the fantail of the ship to float in silent honor of the sacrifice that was once made in that place. After a few minutes, the crew tugged on the line to tip the raft, symbolically reenacting what happened on that tragic July night in 1945. Once again, a sacred cargo slipped into a watery grave. While I was not there, I can vividly imagine the flag and the memorandums sinking into the final resting place of my shipmates. I hope that this act of honorable remembrance will bring comfort to the families who still mourn.

The USS *Indianapolis* Lives On

On January 5, 1980, my wife and I were among a number of other survivors and their wives who celebrated the commissioning of another USS *Indianapolis*—a Los Angeles–class submarine, the USS *Indianapolis* (SSN-697). The official ceremony took place in Groton, Connecticut. Eighteen years later, the *Indianapolis* was decommissioned and stricken from the Naval Vessel Register. The final captain of the *Indianapolis*, William J. Toti, has remained a faithful defender of Captain McVay and is rightly considered part of our family of survivors.

But the legacy of the USS *Indianapolis* did not end there. In August 2013, Secretary of the Navy Ray Mabus sent a very exciting letter to each of the survivors announcing yet another ship to bear the name USS *Indianapolis*.

Dear Mr. Harrell,

The tragic sinking of USS INDIANAPOLIS (CA-35) and struggle for survival in shark-infested waters of nearly 900 crewmembers has long been a testament of enduring courage, determination and resolve in U.S. Naval history. As one of the 317 men who lived through this horrific experience, you and your shipmates alone fully understand how such an experience would ultimately affect your life, just as it affected the Navy as a whole and is to this day woven into the fabric of every Navy Sailor.

As a maritime Nation, our security, our economy and our diplomacy rely upon our freedom of the seas in times of peace and our command of the seas in time of war. We go to the sea in ships and submarines whose names serve as an inspiration to their crew and as a warning to those who would threaten those freedoms we hold most dear. The U.S. Navy has bestowed the name "INDIANAPOLIS" on only one other occasion—a Los Angeles Class submarine that served in commission for 18 years from 1980 to 1998.

To honor the history of your crew, I am pleased to tell you I have notified Congress that, pending authorization and appropriation, I intend to name the next Littoral Combat Ship (LCS) USS *INDIANAPOLIS*. Once again, the name INDIANAPOLIS will be put to sea on the stern of a U.S. Navy warship carrying on the tradition of service that you and your shipmates have forever associated with the name.

A fast, agile surface combatant, the LCS provides the required war fighting capabilities and operational flexibility to execute focused missions close to the shore such as mine warfare, anti-submarine warfare and surface warfare. I sincerely hope you and your family will be able to join in the milestone events that will surround the building and delivery of this fine ship to our Fleet.

Your service to the Navy and the Nation is a testament to the strength of character of Navy Sailors past, present and future. A grateful Navy and a grateful Nation honor that service by sending USS *INDIANAPOLIS* to sea once more.

Sincerely, Ray Mabus

The Miracle of Reconciliation

Often people ask me, "Do you harbor any resentment toward the Japanese for what happened to you and all the others?" The answer is no. But it took time for me to gain a proper perspective.

Over the years I began to realize that the real enemy was not the Japanese soldiers, sailors, and pilots, as barbaric as many of them were. For the most part they were simply pawns on a political chessboard controlled by those in authority over them. Commander Hashimoto and his crew carried out the orders of their emperor, Michinomiya Hirohito (his rule spanned from 1926 until his death in 1989) and his Imperial cabinet that rubber-stamped his every wish. This included Hirohito's desire for a Tripartite Pact with Nazi Germany and Fascist Italy to form the Axis Powers in 1940. As laughable as it may seem, their stated objective was "world peace."

But even if we cast the blame all the way up the chain to the leaders of Japan, Germany, and Italy, we still haven't gone far enough. I believe in good and evil. I believe in God and His enemy, the devil. The sheer evil that was birthed out of these leaders' diabolical pact points to this supernatural enemy. He is the fiend responsible for the death and misery of millions of others, not only in that dreadful war, but all wars throughout history.

Everyone has a theology, whether they know it or not. This is mine, anchored in the Word of God. So my resentment for the Japanese gradually shifted to the real Enemy of men's souls. Man's only hope in triumphing over sin, Satan, and death is in God alone through faith in the Lord Jesus Christ. "For He rescued us from the domain of darkness, and transferred us to the kingdom of His beloved Son, in whom we have redemption, the forgiveness of sins" (Colossians 1:13–14).

Armed with these eternal truths, I was able to let go of resentment and have compassion on my enemies. I learned to pray that God would be merciful to them as He had been to me. I also understood that we are most like God when we forgive, and that harboring malice only gives an enemy prolonged power to inflict pain.

Since then, I have had the privilege to get to know Commander Hashimoto's granddaughter, Atsuko. She and her family

A sweet hug from the great-granddaughter of Commander Hashimoto.

are faithful attendees of every USS *Indianapolis* survivors' reunion. This is an incredible act of courage on their part. But it's important to remember that the atrocities of WWII greatly affected both sides. Hashimoto's family experienced profound loss in that horrific war. The unthinkable happened. The atomic bomb dropped on Hiroshima instantly incinerated all of the commander's family (his granddaughter is the progeny of a second marriage after the war).

At the 2013 reunion, Atsuko and I hugged, and she thanked me for opening my arms and receiving her embrace. She told me she wasn't sure how I would respond. I told her how much it meant to me that she and her family would come to the reunions to honor us and our families. We agreed to build upon this friendship, and we promised to stay in touch.

At Peace

For me, the ordeal of the USS *Indianapolis* will never be over until the Lord takes me home to be with Him. My experiences on board the *Indy* and my anguish of soul while lost at sea remain stunning reminders of the sinfulness of man, the providence of God, and His saving grace. My confident hope will always remain in Him, a sentiment shared by the inspired psalmist who said, "Out of the depths I have cried to You, O Lord. Lord, hear my voice! Let Your ears be attentive to the voice of my supplications. If You, Lord, should mark iniquities, O Lord, who could stand? But there is forgiveness with You, that You may be feared" (Psalm 130:1–4).

Occasionally someone will say to me, "So you were one of the lucky ones. . . ." While I appreciate their kind sentiment, I know in my heart that luck had nothing to do with our rescue.

> I am grateful to my Lord and Savior, Jesus Christ, for bringing me through this ordeal and giving me the strength and willpower to put it behind me and go on with my life.
>
> Survivor Lyle Umenhoffer

In fact, I am convinced that there is no such thing as luck. Our world is not ruled by chance or fate, but by a sovereign God "who works all things after the counsel of His will" (Ephesians 1:11). His providential rule knows no bounds, nor does His omnipotence have limits. For God has said, "The One forming light and creating darkness, causing well-being and creating calamity; I am the LORD who does all these" (Isaiah 45:7).

From the beginning of our creation, God has ordered the events of history to ultimately glorify himself through the person and work of His Son, the Lord Jesus Christ. For "there is salvation in no one else; for there is no other name under heaven that has been given among men by which we must be saved" (Acts 4:12). Every life story either bears witness to His sovereign grace or denies it. But no life has ever been lived apart from the purposes of God. He alone orchestrates the affairs of His creation. Like all the marvelous and mysterious doctrines of God, the coexistence of divine sovereignty and human responsibility remain an incomprehensible paradox to the human mind—certainly one that offends man's rabid commitment to self-determination. But as I look back over my life through the lens of Scripture, I have no doubt that indeed God is in control, and, without coercion, He uses human means to accomplish His purposes—even the sinking of the USS *Indianapolis*. I therefore find solace in the inscrutable mysteries of God and relax in the safety of His sovereign rule. It is to His glory that I recount my story—a story that exalts the One who ultimately authored it.

While I would never claim to know the mind of God, I do claim His promise that He "causes all things to work together for good to those who love God, to those who are called according to His purpose. For those whom He foreknew, He also predestined to become conformed to the image of His Son, so that He would be the firstborn among many brethren; and these whom He predestined, He also called; and these whom He called, He also justified; and these whom He justified, He also glorified" (Romans 8:28–30). With these sacred truths resonating within my heart, I am at peace with what God allowed to happen. And I pray that my testimony to the praise of His glory will inspire many to humble themselves before the Lover of their souls in genuine repentance and place their faith in our Savior, the Lord Jesus Christ. To this end I salute my shipmates, their families, and our friends.

Life is filled with gale force winds that cause the waves to roar;
And like the men of Galilee we strain against the oar.

With billows high we cry aloud, "Oh, Lord, where have you gone?"
Then He whispers through the squall, "I've been here all along."

Oh we of little faith, why doubt? Why give our hearts to fear?
For when the tempest trials blow, 'tis then we must draw near!

For in the wind of every storm a Sovereign eye doth see,
The waning faith and broken hearts of those like you and me.

And with His outstretched hand of love, He reaches down to save,
All who trust in Him alone; for us His life He gave!

So when the tumults o'er us roll, let's thank Him for the gale,
For in His love He caused the storm, 'twas He who set the sail.

by David Harrell
derived from an exposition of Matthew 14:22-33

"The Navy Hymn"

Eternal Father, strong to save,
Whose arm hath bound the restless wave,
Who bid'st the mighty ocean deep
Its own appointed limits keep;
O hear us when we cry to Thee,
For those in peril on the sea!

O Christ! Whose voice the waters heard
And hushed their raging at Thy word,
Who walked'st on the foaming deep,
And calm amidst its rage didst sleep;
O hear us when we cry to Thee,
For those in peril on the sea!

Most Holy Spirit! Who didst brood
Upon the chaos dark and rude,
And bid its angry tumult cease,
And give, for wild confusion, peace;
O hear us when we cry to Thee,
For those in peril on the sea!

O Trinity of love and power!
Our brethren shield in danger's hour;
From rock and tempest, fire and foe,
Protect them wheresoe'er they go;
Thus evermore shall rise to Thee
Glad hymns of praise from land and sea.

The "Navy Hymn" is also known as "Eternal Father, Strong to Save." The original words were written as a poem in 1860 by clergyman William Whiting of Winchester, England, for a student who was about to sail for the United States. The melody, published in 1861, was composed by fellow English clergyman John B. Dykes.

The hymn, found in most hymnals, is known as the "Navy Hymn" because it is sung at the U.S. Naval Academy in Annapolis, Maryland. It is also sung on ships of the Royal Navy (UK) and has been translated into French.

"Eternal Father," said to be President Franklin Roosevelt's favorite hymn, was sung at his funeral. It was also played by the Navy Band in 1963 as President John F. Kennedy's body was carried up the steps of the U.S. Capitol to lie in state. Roosevelt had served as Secretary of the Navy and Kennedy was a PT (patrol torpedo) boat commander in World War II.[1]

The "Marines' Hymn"

From the halls of Montezuma
To the shores of Tripoli;
We fight our country's battles
In the air, on land, and sea.

First to fight for right and freedom,
And to keep our honor clean;
We are proud to claim the title
Of United States Marine.

Our flag's unfurled to every breeze
From dawn to setting sun;
We have fought in every clime and place
Where we could take a gun.

In the snow of far-off northern lands
And in sunny tropic scenes;
You will find us always on the job—
The United States Marines.

Here's health to you and to our Corps
Which we are proud to serve;

In many a strife we've fought for life
And never lost our nerve.

If the Army and the Navy
Ever look on Heaven's scenes;
They will find the streets are guarded
By United States Marines.

Notes

Chapter 1: A Call to Arms

1. Mochitsura Hashimoto, *Sunk: The Story of the Japanese Submarine Fleet, 1942–1945* (New York: Henry Holt, 1954), 57.

2. Patrick J. Finneran, "The Tragedy of the USS *Indianapolis* (CA-35)," 1994, The USS *Indianapolis* (CA-35) Survivors' Organization, www.ussindianapolis.org/pfinnstory.htm.

3. Ibid.

4. Daniel E. Brady, of the V (Aviation) Division, personal account in Patrick J. Finneran's article, "The Tragedy of the USS *Indianapolis* (CA-35)," 1994, www.ussindianapolis.org/pfinnstory.htm.

Chapter 2: The *Indy Maru*

1. Katherine D. Moore, *Good-bye,* Indy Maru (Knoxville, TN: Lori Publications, 1991), 52.

2. *Dictionary of American Naval Fighting Ships, Vol. III* (Washington, D.C.: Navy Department, 1968), 434.

3. Ibid., 435.

4. Ibid.

5. Ibid.

6. Ibid.

7. Ibid.

8. Doug Stanton, *In Harm's Way* (New York: Henry Holt, 2001), 37.

9. Patrick J. Finneran.

Chapter 3: Tragedy Explodes—the First Day

1. Stanton, 73–75.
2. Ibid., 78.
3. Ibid., 77.
4. Ibid., 86.
5. Raymond Lech, *All the Drowned Sailors* (New York: Stein and Day, 1982), 31.
6. Richard Newcomb, *Abandon Ship! Death of the USS* Indianapolis (Bloomington: Indiana University Press, 1958), 57.
7. Hashimoto, 172.
8. Newcomb, 8.
9. Hashimoto, 177.
10. Newcomb, 8.
11. Hashimoto, 220.
12. Ibid., 221–225.
13. Stanton, 172.

Chapter 4: Mysteries of Darkness and Light—the Second Day

1. Ibid., 180–182.

Chapter 6: Ducks on the Pond—the Fourth Day

1. L. Peter Wren, *We Were There: The USS* Indianapolis *Tragedy* (Richmond, VA: L. Peter Wren, 2002), 11.
2. Stanton, 216.
3. Ibid., 211–216.
4. Ibid., 219.
5. Ibid., 225.
6. Ibid., 25–30.
7. Lieutenant Marks recorded his memories in a booklet he authored, *Selected Speeches of R. Adrian Marks* (1990).
8. Ibid., 225–226.
9. R. Adrian Marks, *Selected Speeches of R. Adrian Marks* (Survivors' Reunion, 1990), 32.
10. Ibid., 34.
11. Ibid., 36–39.
12. Ibid., 39–41.

Chapter 7: Tragedy and Triumph—the Fifth Day

1. Stanton, 239.

2. L. Peter Wren, *Those in Peril on the Sea* (Richmond, VA: L. Peter Wren, 1999), 162.

3. Stanton, 239.

4. Reported by Grace Schneider, *Journal and Courier* (Lafayette, IN), date unknown.

5. Ibid., 253.

6. *The Paris Intelligence*, March 16, 1994.

7. Marks, 53.

8. Ibid., 45–46.

9. Ibid., 44.

Chapter 8: Journey for Justice

1. Dan Kurzman, *Fatal Voyage: The Sinking of the USS* Indianapolis (New York: Atheneum, 1990), 202.

2. Ibid., 204–206.

3. Ibid.

4. *The Sinking of USS* Indianapolis: *Navy Department Press Release Charges and Specifications in Case of Capt. Charles B. McVay, III, USN, 3 Dec. 1945,* www.history.navy.mil/faqs/faq30-2.htm.

5. Ibid.

6. Newcomb, 252.

7. Kurzman, 212–213.

8. Newcomb, 252.

9. Hunter Scott, "Timeline to Justice," *Naval History*, July–August 1998.

10. "Language of the Legislation," The USS *Indianapolis* (CA-35) Survivors' Organization, www.ussindianapolis.org.

The Navy Hymn

1. Navy Hymn information adapted from LindaJo H. McKim, *The Presbyterian Hymnal Companion* (Louisville, KY: Westminster/John Knox Press, 1993), 377, and Naval History and Command website, http://www.history.navy.mil/faqs/faq53-1.htm.

Other Resources

Saved By a Substitute
In his twelve-page booklet, former Navy petty officer O. Talmadge Spence describes a fascinating account of how "the merciful providence of God" prevented him from boarding the doomed USS *Indianapolis* by only two hours, and ultimately led him to a saving faith in the Lord Jesus Christ. Dr. Spence later became the founder and president of Foundations Bible College in Dunn, North Carolina. For more information, visit www.foundations.edu/bookstore/item_details.php?Section=Misc&ItemNum=85.

Only 317 Survived!
This is a fascinating book of personal testimonies written by 102 survivors of the USS *Indianapolis* and forty deceased survivors' families. Each personal recollection reminds the reader of the triumph of courage and the enormous sacrifice that was made for our freedom.

About the Authors

Edgar Harrell, USMC (Ret.), owned and operated a distributorship for the Pella Window Company in Rock Island, Illinois, for thirty-five years, served for fifteen years on the board of the Moody Bible Institute, and has been a lay minister throughout his adult life. He lives in Clarksville, Tennessee, with his wife, Ola, enjoying their two children, eight grandchildren, and eight great-grandchildren. Edgar speaks extensively around the United States about his survival at sea.

David Harrell is currently the senior pastor-teacher of Calvary Bible Church (www.cbctn.org), where he has served since 1997. His Bible expositions are heard and read regularly around the world over the Internet and broadcasted over the radio. He is also the president of Olive Tree Christian Resources (www.otcr .org), which serves as the media arm of Calvary Bible Church, committed to the creation and distribution of Christian books, expository sermons, Internet and radio programming, websites for doctrinally sound evangelical churches, pastoral training, and church planting. After attending the Moody Bible Institute, he graduated from Grace College, Grace Theological Seminary, and the Oxford Graduate School where he earned a Doctor of Philosophy degree in social research methods, which focuses on the sociological integration of religion and society. He is a former associate professor of Biblical counseling at the Master's College, Santa Clarita, California. He is married to Nancy, and together they have three children and six grandchildren.